BLUES HARMONICA

COLLECTION

BY DAVID McKELVY

THE GOODMAN GROUP
Music Publishers
New York, New York
Exclusively Distributed by
Hal Leonard Publishing Corporation
7777 West Bluemound Road P.O. Box 13819 Milwaukee, WI 53213

ISBN 0-7935-1600-5

INTRODUCTION

With the advent of amplified playing using the low-wattage amps in the late '40s/early '50s, the blues harmonica could finally be heard alongside other instruments. The harmonica was no longer overpowered as it had been in acoustic settings. In accompanying style as well as solo styles, the harp began to function as a "horn." Phrasings begin to swing a bit more, syncopation became more interesting and a new breed of players was born...

LITTLE WALTER (Walter Jacobs)

Little Walter is considered by many aficionados of Chicago-style blues harmonica to have been the greatest of all players. At the very least, he was far and away the most innovative player of his time.

Although Little Walter's playing showed the influence of other players, including Sonny Boy Williamson, his style gradually evolved into something completely original and apart from that of his predecessors. With the increased use of low-wattage amps, his playing sounded more sax-like and less like a traditional harmonica. His phrasing became more horn-like, and freer and jazzier. His use of octaves and other split tonguings, as well as his ability to switch from deep to shallow throat tones, was amazing and continues to influence succeeding generations of Chicago-style blues harp players everywhere.

SONNY BOY WILLIAMSON (Aleck "Rice" Miller)

Sonny Boy Williamson was most influential in effecting a transition from country acoustic styles to big city, amplified modes of blues harmonica playing. He was not a particularly notey player; his trademark was the economy with which he used short riffs and rhythm patterns to help define each song. His tongue rhythm technique remains unsurpassed.

The later recordings are marked by the use of longer notes with more fluid and developed melodic lines. Perhaps the most significant aspect of his artistry was the irony, humor and sheer intensity with which he wrote, sang and played the blues.

HOWLIN' WOLF (Chester Burnett)

Because of his devilish behavior, Burnett's father dubbed him "Wolf." His harmonica style, though not elaborate, was very effective at the gut level at which the blues exists. His phrases, riffs and turnarounds served to underscore some of the most emotionally-inspired blues vocals ever. Indeed, Howlin' Wolf was known primarily as a vocalist, but his blues harp sang out as an added voice on some of the greatest blues performances ever recorded.

JIMMY REED

Although known primarily for his singing and songwriting, Jimmy Reed's harmonica playing was unique and continues to influence harmonica players, particularly those who play straight harp. For the most part, Reed played his harmonica on a rack around his neck, while he played guitar. In spite of this seemingly awkward approach, his notes were clear, well-controlled and very effective.

In particular, his trademark style of playing the blow-bends on the high end of the harp were amazing for a *rack* player. His solos were simple, his riffs short, every note meant alot. Any student of straight-harp blues playing could do no better than to study Reed. Of any of the writers in this book, his songs had the most "hooks" — catch phrases, both lyrically and melodically. This helped him reach a wider commercial audience than most blues artists.

CONTENTS

BLUES HARMONICA • ALPHABETICAL AND BY ARTIST

HOW TO READ THE HARMONICA TABLATURE
TERMS AND SYMBOLS

One of the best ways to become an accomplished player on blues harmonica is to learn the solos and fills from recordings of the great blues harp masters. In this book, you'll find some of the most famous solos in note-for-note transcriptions in both music notation and harmonica tablature.

The tablature system for the harmonica parts is simple:

For each note, you are given the number of the hole to be played followed by an arrow pointing up ↑ to indicate a **blow** note (↑), or an arrow pointing down ↓ to indicate a **draw** note (↓), (e.g., 4 ↑ = blow hole 4).

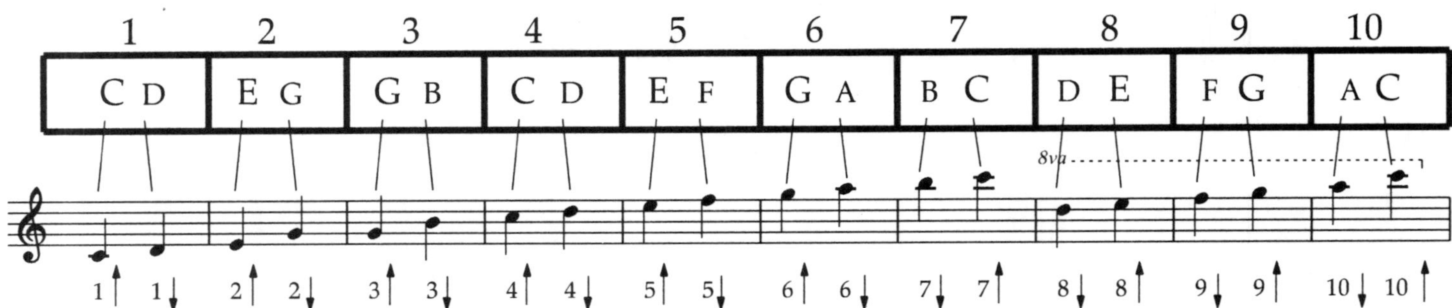

BENDING NOTES

Lowering the pitch of a note by bending is indicated by a bent arrow following the hole number. The angle of the bend in the arrow indicates the degree to which the note is bent. Bent notes are indicated as follows (music notation examples here are for a C harmonica);

Draw Bends:

The draw notes on holes 1, 4 and 6 (1 ↓, 4 ↓ & 6 ↓) can be bent down only a half-step, so the only bend symbol used on these holes is: 1 ↵, 4 ↵, 6 ↵

2 draw (2 ↓)

can be bent a half-step

indicated by 2 ↙

or a whole step,

indicated by 2 ↵

3 draw (3 ↓)

can be bent down a half-step

indicated by 3 ↙

or a whole step,

indicated by 3 ↵

or three half-steps,

indicated by 3 ↘

Blow Bends:

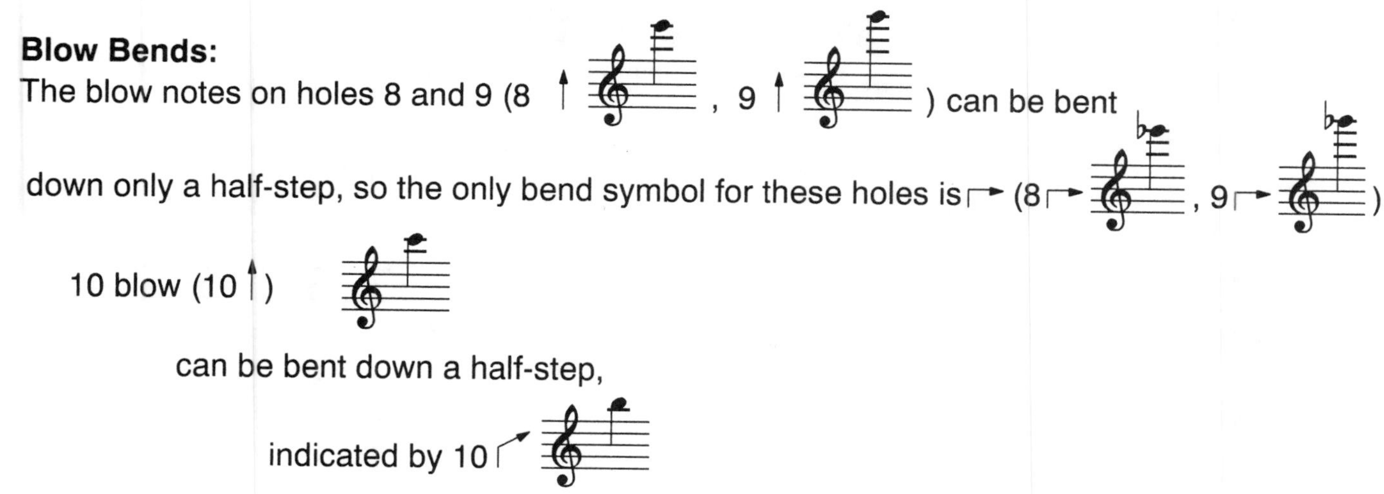

The blow notes on holes 8 and 9 (8 ↑, 9 ↑) can be bent down only a half-step, so the only bend symbol for these holes is ↱ (8↱, 9↱).

10 blow (10 ↑)

can be bent down a half-step,

indicated by 10↗

or a whole step,

indicated by 10↱

Here are some of the terms and symbols used in this book:

STRAIGHT HARP ("first position"): Means playing in the key stamped on the harmonica. For example, playing in the key of C on a C harmonica.

CROSS HARP ("second position"): Playing in the key a fourth below the key stamped on the harmonica. For example, playing in the key of G on a C harmonica, or in the key of A on a D harmonica. This is the most often used position for playing blues style harmonica.

DORIAN MODE ("third position"): Playing in the key a second above the key of the harmonica. For example, playing in the key of D on a C harmonica, or in the key of E on a D harmonica.

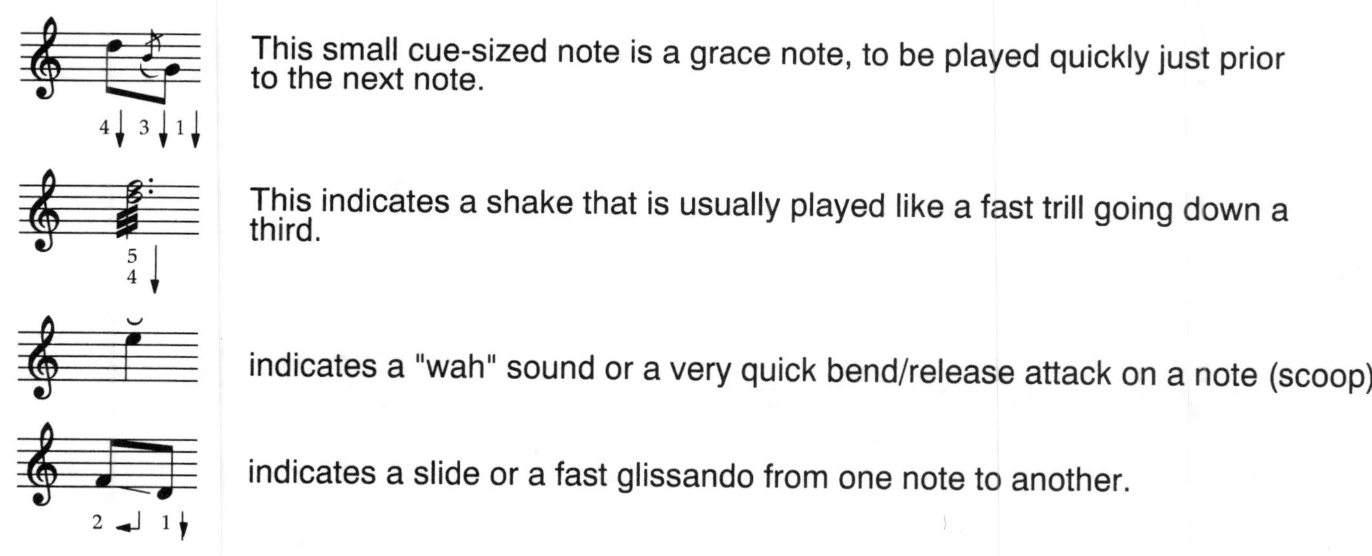

This small cue-sized note is a grace note, to be played quickly just prior to the next note.

This indicates a shake that is usually played like a fast trill going down a third.

indicates a "wah" sound or a very quick bend/release attack on a note (scoop).

indicates a slide or a fast glissando from one note to another.

8va — indicates to play up one octave.

8vb — indicates to play down one octave.

It is important to listen to the recordings from which this book was transcribed. In addition to the original Lps and cassettes, many of these recordings are now being reissued on CD.

Listen to these recordings for tone, phrasing, inflection and, in particular, the way in which the harp is used in the context of the overall performances.

Harmonica key of C

All My Love In Vain

By Sonny Boy Williamson

Cross harp

G
vain, __ 2↓ 2 2↑ 2↓ 3 2↓ 2 1↓ 2↓ 1↓ but the
D7 C7
peo - ple's al - ways told me that a wom - an was the glor - y of a man. ___
G D7
__ 3↑ 2↑ 2↓ 2↓ 2↓ 2↓ 2↓ 2↓ 3↑ 1↓ 1↓ If you
G C7
whip her ____ when she need it, the judge will not let you ex -
G G7
plain. _____ 4↓ 4 3↓ 2↓ 3↑ 3↓ 4↓ 5↓ 5↓ 5↓ 4↓ 3↓ 2↓
C7
Whip her when she need it, the judge will not let you ex -
G
plain, __ 3↓ 2↓ 2 2↑ 2↓ 3 2↓ 2 1↓ be - cause he be -
D7 C7
lieve in jus - tice and a wom - an is the glor - y of a man.

D7
Solo
G
G7
C7
G
D7
C7
G
D7
G
I'd ra - ther be tied out on the des - ert.
C7
G
right out in the fall - ing rain.
G7
C7
Tied out on the des - ert

G
right out in the fall - ing rain,
D7
than to lose my ba - by,
C7
G7
she is the glor - y of a man.
D7
Solo
G
G7
C7
G
D7
C7
G

Harmonica key of C

Cross harp

Ah'w Baby

By Walter Jacobs

Slow shuffle

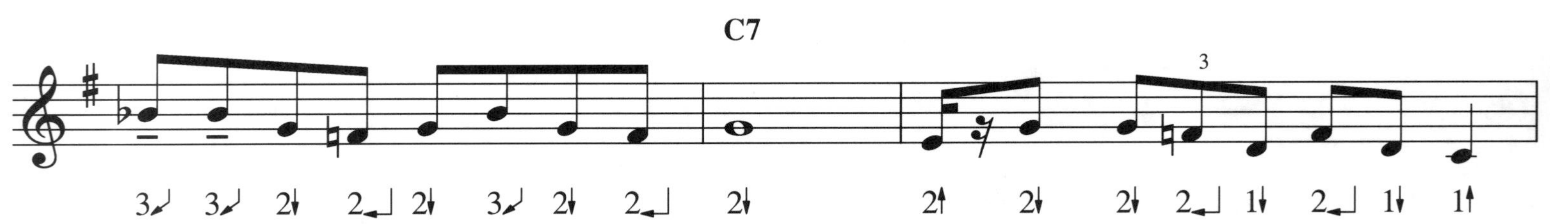

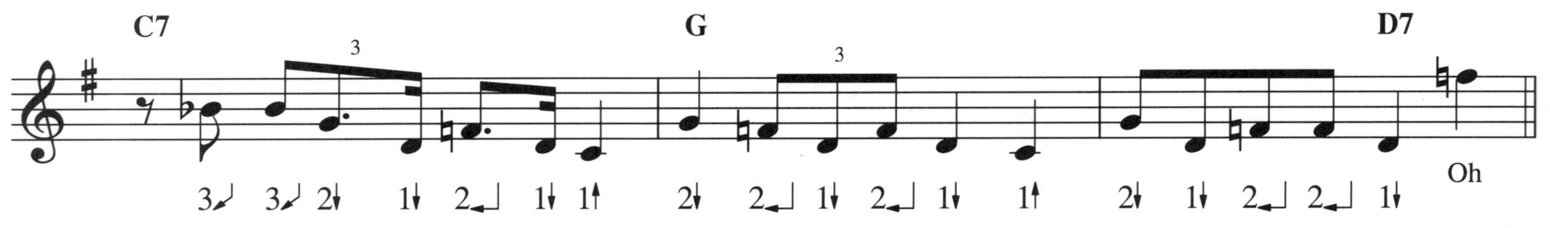

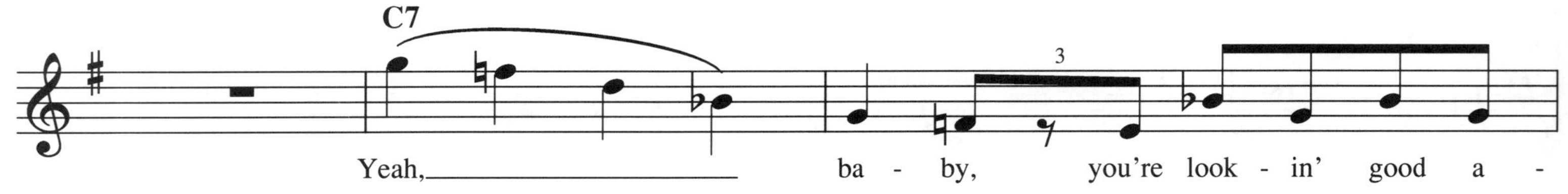

G
D7
gain to - night. ______
You were made for me ba - by,
C7
G
D7
I can't wait 'til to - mor - row night. ______
Oh,
G
ba - by,
I want to will my love to you, ______
C7
Whoa ___ yeah, ______
I want to will my love to you. ______
G
D7
You are my kind of ba - by, ______
C7
G
D7
ba - by you's the one I choose. ______
G
3↓ 4↓ 5↓ 5↓ 2↓
4↓ 5↓ 6↑ 5↓ 4↓ 4↑ 4↓ 3↓ 4↑ 3↑ 2↑ 2↓ 2 1↓
2↓ 2↓ 3↑ 2↓ 2↓
C7
4↓ 5↓ 4↓
3↓ 4↓ 5↑ 5↓ 5↑ 4↓ 5↑ 5↓ 5↑ 4↓ 5↑ 5↓ 5↑ 4↓ 5↑

G
5↓ 5↑4↓ 5↑ 5↓ 5↑4↓ 4↑ 3↓ 3 2↓ 2↑ 2 1↓ 2↓ 3↓ 2↓ 3↓ 5↓ 6↑ 5↓

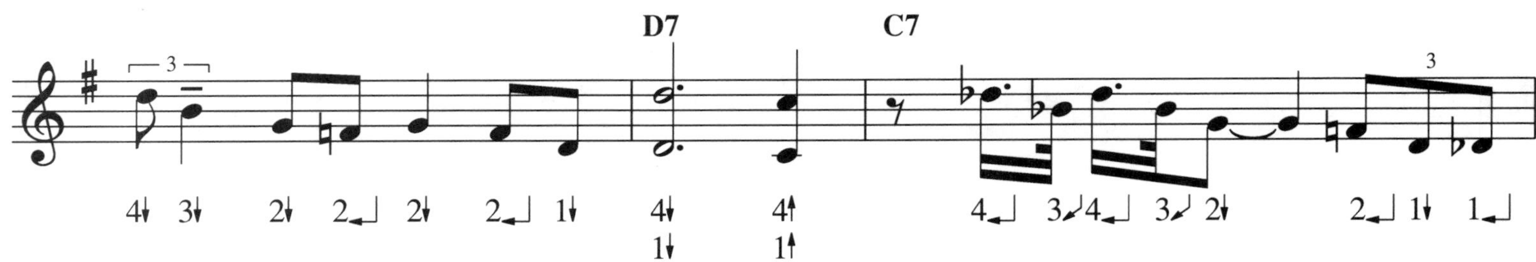
D7 C7
4↓ 3↓ 2↓ 2 2↓ 2 1↓ 4↓ 1↓ 4↑ 1↑ 4 3 4 3 2↓ 2 1↓ 1

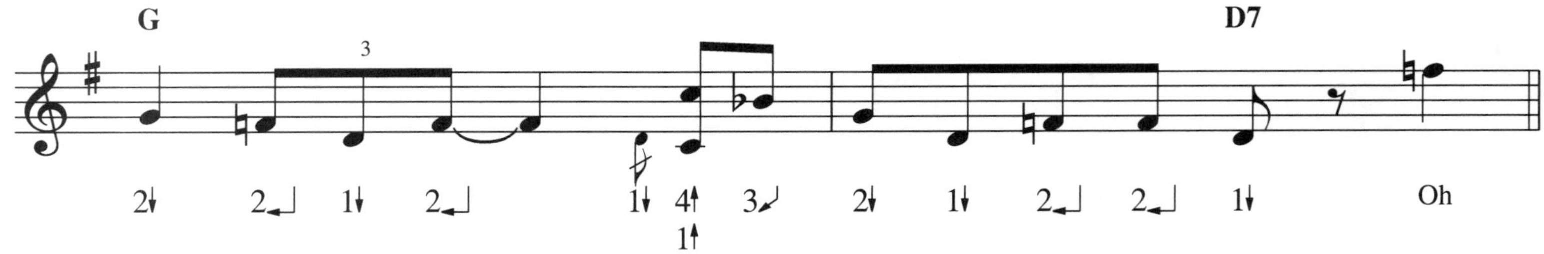
G D7
2↓ 2 1↓ 2 1↓ 4↑ 1↑ 3 2↓ 1↓ 2 2 1↓
Oh

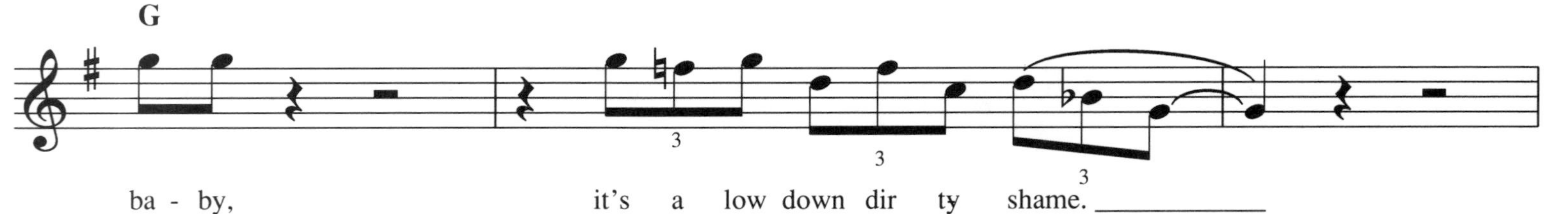
G
ba - by, it's a low down dir ty shame.

C7
Oh yeah, a low down dir - ty shame.

G D7 C7
Bad way they talk a - bout you, but I love you just the same.

G
3↑ 2↑ 3↓ 2↓ 2↓ 4↑ 3↓ 2↓ 3↓ 2↓ 4↑ 3↓ 2↓ 2 1↓ 2↓ 2↓

Boom, Boom Out Go The Lights

Harmonica key of A

By Stan Lewis

Cross harp

B
E
B
E
A
E
B
E
B
E
A
E
B7
E
B

E
A
Am
E
B
D.S. al Coda
E
B
Coda
B
E
B
E
A
E
B
fade ending

Baby What You Want Me To Do

By Jimmy Reed

Harmonica key of B♭

Cross harp

Moderately slow shuffle
guitar intro

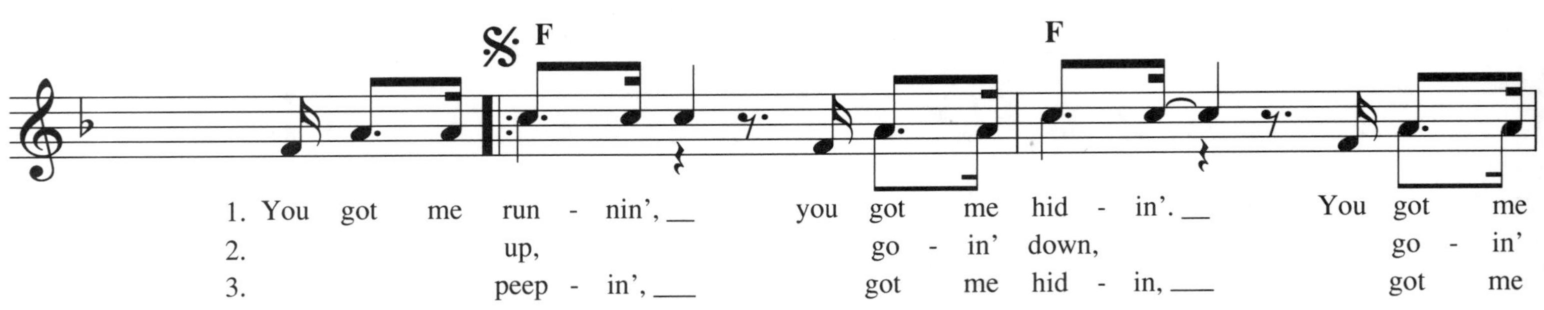

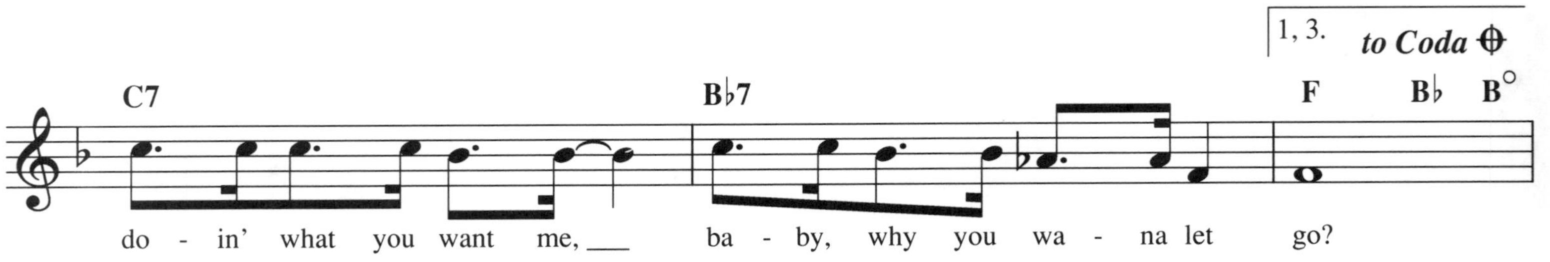

F
C7
2. Go - in'
2.
F
go.
Solo
C7
F
B♭7
F
C7
B♭7
F
C7
D.S. al Coda
3. Got me
Coda
F
C7
F
fade ending

Harmonica key of B♭

Cross harp

Back Track

By Walter Jacobs

F7
B♭7
F
C7
B♭7
F
C7
F
F7
B♭7
F
C7
B♭7
F
C7
F
F7
B♭7
F

C7 B♭7 F C7
F F7
B♭7 F
C7 B♭7 F C7
F
F7 B♭7 F
C7 B♭7 F
C7 F

F7
B♭7
F
C7
B♭7
F
C7
F
F7
B♭7
F
C7
B♭7
F
C7
F
F7

Harmonica key of D

Cross harp

Blues With A Feeling

By Walter Jacobs

1.
Solo E7
A
D7
A
E7
D7
A
E7
2.
A7
Well, you know I love you, ba - by, I won - der the rea - son why; you
told me you loved me ba - by and you left me here to cry.
D.S. 𝄋 First Verse al Coda
Coda
A
A7
day.

Harmonica key of A

Straight harp

Bright Lights, Big City

By Jimmy Reed

Verse 2:
Go ahead, pretty baby,
honey, knock yourself out.
Go ahead, pretty baby,
honey, knock yourself out.
I still love you, baby, 'cause you
don't know what it's all about.

Chorus 2:
Bright lights, big city
went to my baby's head.
Bright lights, big city
went to my baby's head.

fade ending

Harmonica key of C

Cross harp

Can't Hold Out Much Longer

By Walter Jacobs

just nap through the day; I can't hold on much long - er Lord
G7
C7
liv - in' this a - way You know I'm cra - zy 'bout you ba - by,
G
won - der do you ev - er think of me?
D7
You know I'm in love with you, dar - lin' but you
C7
G
don't care noth - ing in the world for me.
D7
Solo
G
C7
G
G7
C7

G
D7
C7
G
D7
G
Now, there ain't but the one thing, ba - by, real - ly
makes your dad - dy drink;
you say that you don't love me, Lord, and
G7
C7
I be - gin to think. You know I'm cra - zy 'bout you ba - by,
wom - an do you ev - er think of me?
G
You know I'm just
D7
wild a - bout you, ba - by, but you
C7
G
don't care noth - ing in the world for me.

Harmonica key of E

Cool Disposition

Cross harp

By Sonny Boy Williamson

B
She got me pret - ty please,
peo-ples, I just can't sleep at night.
E7
Got me pret-ty please,
B
you know boys, I just can't sleep at night.
I don't eat
F#7
E7
my break-fast in the morn-ing
and my teeth and tongue be - gin to fight.
B
F#7
Solo
B
B7
E7
B

F♯7
E7
B
F♯7
Yes, she's
B
E7
for - ty - one through the shoul-ders,
twen - ty - nine __ in the waist. _
B
I'll nev - er find __ an - oth - er wom - an to take my ba - by's place; she's so
E7
love - ly,
she's so ____ sweet, __ she's so kind. _
B
She's got such a
F♯7
E7
cool dis - po - si-tion,
makes _ me __ love her all the
B
time.

Harmonica key of D

Checkin' Up On My Baby

Cross harp

By Sonny Boy Willamson

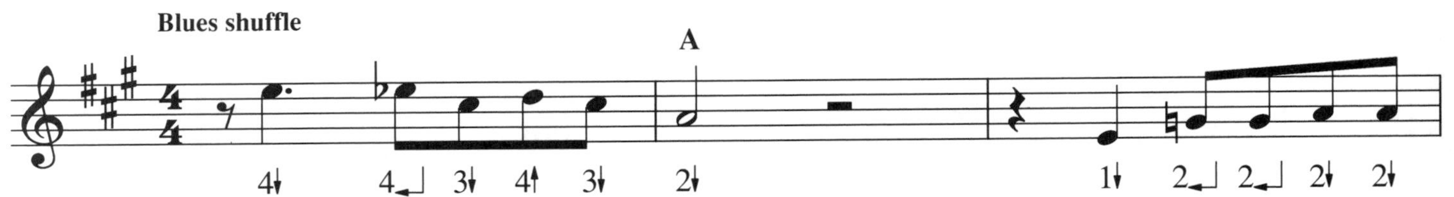

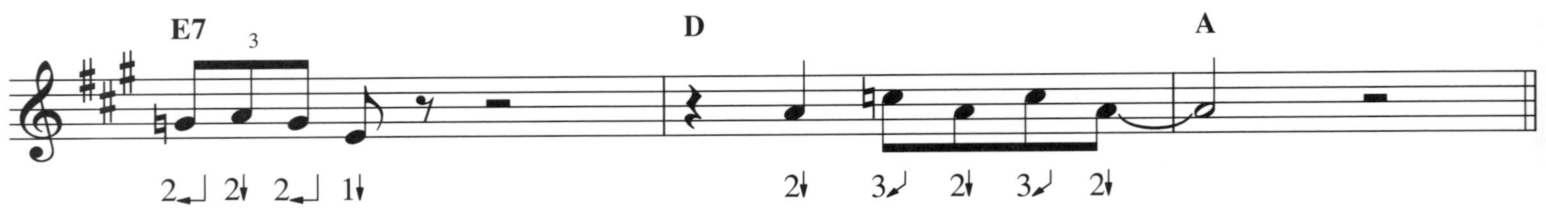

A
trying' to find out what she put - tin' down.
So man-y nights and days _
E7
D
A
you know I have been out of town.
I'm a - fraid to write a let-ter, ___
I would-n't ev - en make no tel - e-phone
call.
D
I'm a - fraid to write a let - ter, ____
A
I did-n't make no tel - e-phone call;
'cause I did-n't want my ba -
E7
D
A
by __
to know I was back in town at all. ____
E7
A

D
2↓ 4↓ 4↓ 4↓ 4↓ 4↓ 4↓ 4 3↓ 4↑ 2↓ 3↓ 4↑
A
2↓ 3 2↓ 3 2↓ 3 2↓ 2↓ 2↓ 2↓ 2↓ 3 2↓ 3 2↓
E7
D
A
2↓ 2 1↓ 2↓ 3 2↓ 3 2↓ 3↓ 2↓ 2↓
I would-n't e-ven call no-bod-y,
I would-n't e-ven be seen;
I did-n't talk to no-
D
A
bod-y and I did-n't want to be seen.
E7
D
I want to sleep off all my pit-y as a mid-night

A
E7
A
dream.
Check-in', check-in' on my ba-by, ___
try - in' to find out what she put - tin' down. __
D
Check - in' up on my ba - by,
A
try - in' to find out what she put - tin' down. __
E7
Be - cause I been a long time ______
D
A
E7
since _ I been back in town. __
A
Repeat to fade ending

Cross My Heart

By Sonny Boy Williamson

Harmonica key of F

Cross harp

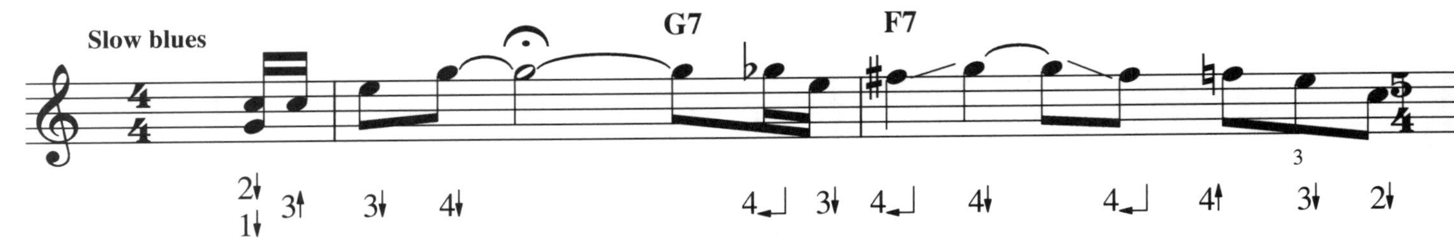

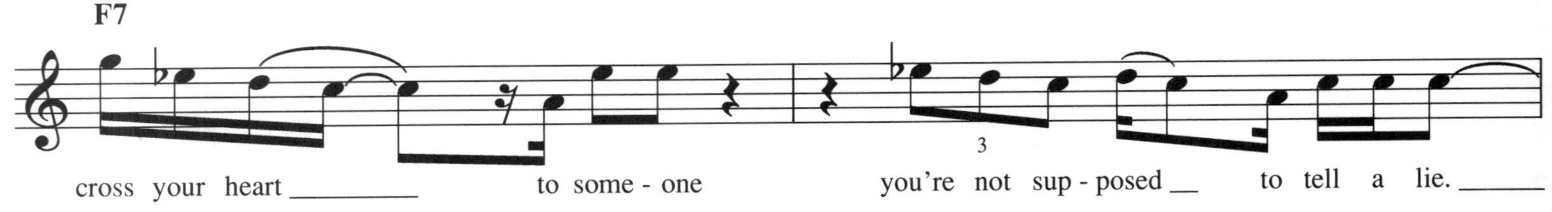

G7 C
The first time I crossed my heart
F7 C C7
I was by your bed - side on my knees. Yes,
F7
the first time I crossed my heart. I was by your bed - side down on my
C G7
knees. Sure 'nough man. And I know the dif - 'frence be - tween I and
F7 C
you I have to beg you please dar - ling help me, please.
G7 Solo C F7
C C7 F7

C
G7
F7
C
C
G7
C
I cross my heart
F7
C
C7
for you and to no - one else I know.
I cross my
F7
heart true to you that you a ba - by be - cause I know there's no one else I
C
G7
know.
An - y - thing you tell me to do I have done,
F7
C
F7
C
do it or I'll have to go.

Harmonica key of E

Don't Lose Your Eye

By Sonny Boy Williamson

Cross harp

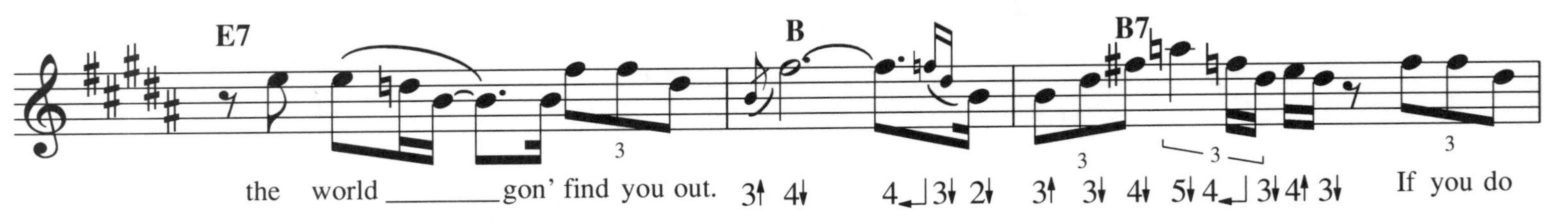
E7
B
B7
the world ________ gon' find you out.
If you do

E7
B
wrong, __ dar - ling per - son,
the world __ gon' find you out.

F♯7
You know you can't do wrong and get by, _____

E7
B
an - y - thing you try _____
to dodge ___ they'll doubt. _____

F♯7
B
E7
If I was you,
I'd play fair in an - y - thing I do.

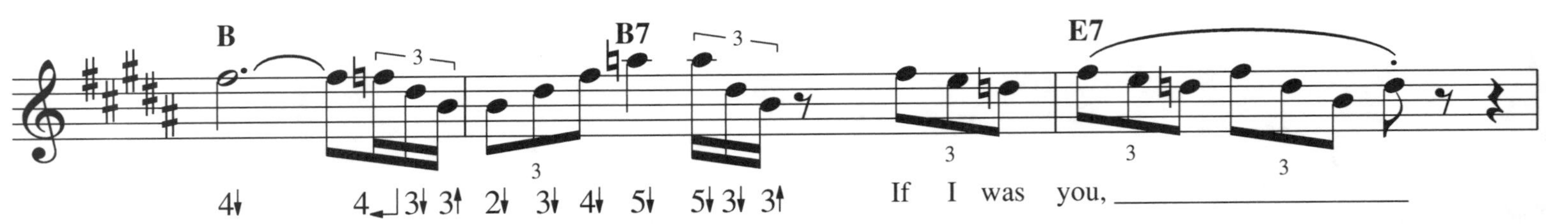
B
B7
E7
If I was you, ____________________

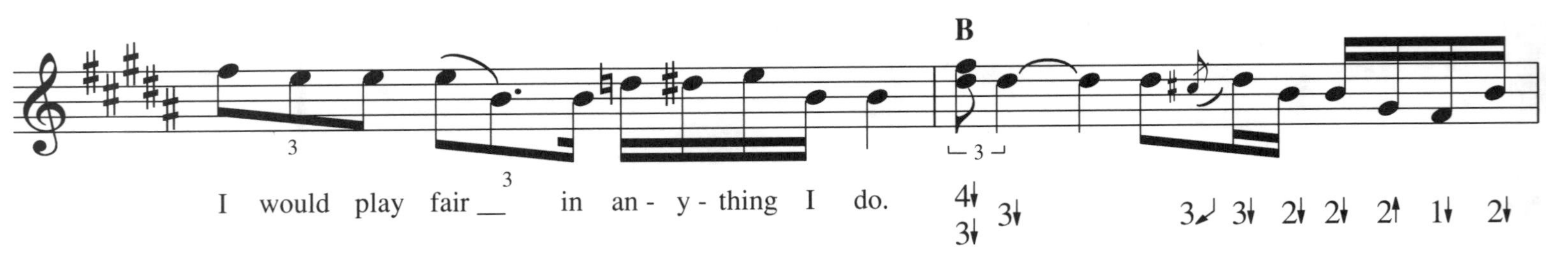
B
I would play fair __ in an - y - thing I do.

F♯7
An - y - time the peo - ple find out that you're crook - ed, man, they're not gon'
E7
B
F♯7
do noth - in' in the world for you,
B
E7
My dad - dy taught me, whoa - man, since I was a child.
B
B7
E7
My dad - dy taught me,
ev - er since I was a child,
B
Al - ways
F♯7
E7
B
treat your neigh - bor right, be fair with your friends like wise.
F♯7
Fade

Harmonica key of C

Don't Start Me Talkin'

By Sonny Boy Williamson

Cross harp

G C7 G C7
and get some mar - ket. Gets out on the streets,
G C7 G C7
Ol' George stopped her he knocked her down,
G C7 G
and black - ened her eye. She gets back home tell her
G7 C7
hus - band a lie. Don't start me talk - in',
G
I'll tell ev - 'ry - thing I know.
4↓ 4↓ 4↓ 4↓ 4↓ 4↓ 4↓ 4↓
D7
4 3↓ 4↑ 5↑ 3↓ 4↑ 2↓ 2
3↑ 4↑ 2↓ 3↑
I'm gon' break up this sig - ni - fyin',
C7 G D7
some bod - y's got to go.
2↓ 2↓ 2↓ 2↓ 2↓ 2↓ 1↓ 1↓
Solo G
2↓ 2↓ 2↓ 2↓ 2↓ 2↓ 2↓ 2↓ 2↓ 2↓ 2↓ 2↓ 2↓ 2↓ 2↓ 2↓ 2↓ 2↓ 2↓

G7
C7
3
2 2 2 2 2 2
4 4
4
4 3 4
3 3
G
D7
3
3 4 4 3 4 4 3 4 4 3 5
4
3
4 3 4 4 3 4 4 3 4 4 3 4
3
2
4
C7
G
3
3
D7
4 4 3
3 2 3 2 2 1 1
2 1 1
G
C7
G
C7
3
3
She bor - rowed some mon - ey,
go to the beau - ty shop.
G
C7
G
C7
He honked his horn,
she be - gun to stop.
G
C7
G
C7
Said, "Take me, ba - by,
a - round the block.
I'm
G
C7
G
G7
3
3
gon' to the beau - ty shop, where I can
get my hair a chop." Don't

C7
start me talk - in'. I'll tell ev - 'ry - thing I
G
know.
Well,
D7
C7
break up this sig - ni - fy - in, oh
some - bod - y's got to go.
G
D7
G
C7
G
D7
C7
G

Harmonica key of F

Cross harp

Down Child

By Sonny Boy Williamson

C
F7
time she smiles, says she don't love no one but
C
you. Ev - 'ry
F7
time she smiles, says she don't love no one but
C
you. You
G
F7
bet - ter watch out bud - dy boy, lit - tle girl, love to drop a chunk on
C
G7
Solo
C
you.
C7
F7

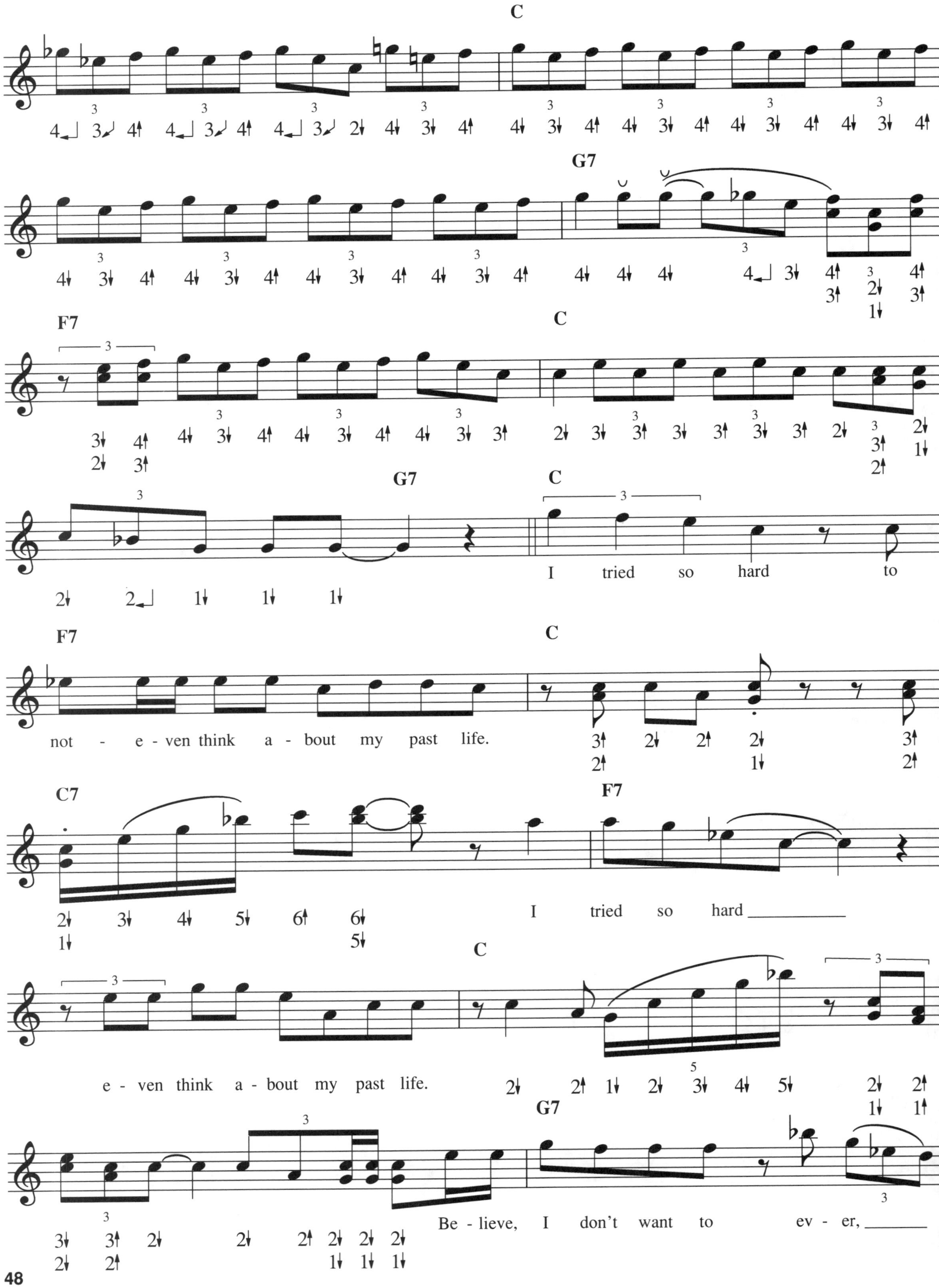

C

4↲ 3↙ 4↑ 4↲ 3↙ 4↑ 4↲ 3↙ 2↓ 4↓ 3↓ 4↑ 4↓ 3↓ 4↑ 4↓ 3↓ 4↑ 4↓ 3↓ 4↑ 4↓ 3↓ 4↑

G7

4↓ 3↓ 4↑ 4↓ 3↓ 4↑ 4↓ 3↓ 4↑ 4↓ 3↓ 4↑ 4↓ 4↓ 4↓ 4↲ 3↓ 4↑/3↑ 2↓/1↓ 4↑/3↑

F7 C

3↓/2↓ 4↑/3↑ 4↓ 3↓ 4↑ 4↓ 3↓ 4↑ 4↓ 3↓ 3↑ 2↓ 3↓ 3↑ 3↓ 3↑ 3↓ 3↑ 2↓ 3↑/2↑ 2↓/1↓

G7 C

2↓ 2↲ 1↓ 1↓ 1↓

I tried so hard to

F7 C

not - e - ven think a - bout my past life.

3↑/2↑ 2↓ 2↑ 2↓/1↓ 3↑/2↑

C7 F7

2↓/1↓ 3↓ 4↓ 5↓ 6↑ 6↓/5↓

I tried so hard ______

C

e - ven think a - bout my past life.

2↓ 2↑ 1↓ 2↓ 3↓ 4↓ 5↓ 2↓/1↓ 2↑/1↑

G7

3↓/2↓ 3↑/2↑ 2↓ 2↓ 2↑ 2↓/1↓ 2↓/1↓ 2↓/1↓

Be - lieve, I don't want to ev - er, ______

F7 C
ev - er make a a mis - take in life.
G7 C
Ba - by, I and you could be so hap - py,
F7 C
we can be so lov - in' to - night. From now on
F7
dar - ling, yeah, we can be so hap - py,
C
be so lov - ey, from now on, from now on.
G7
Be - cause if I ev - er make a mis - take in life,
F7 C G7
I know I'd ruin my hap - py home. Whoa.
C F7
C C7 F7
Fade

Harmonica key of E

Fattening Frogs For Snakes

Cross harp

By Sonny Boy Williamson

E7
B
F♯7
E7
B
F♯7
B
I found out my down - fall,
E7
B
E7
back in nine - teen and thir - ty.
(I started checking) I found out my down - fall
B
in nine - teen and thir - ty,
F♯7
E7
I'm tel - ling all of my friends I'm not fat - tnin' no more frogs for
B
F♯7
Solo
B
snakes,
(All right now)
B7

E7
B
F♯7
E7

B
F♯7
B
Yes it's nine - teen and fif - ty - sev - en;

E7
B
B7
I've got to cor - rect all of my mis - takes.
Whoa, man,

E7
nine - teen and fif - ty - sev - en; I've got to cor - rect all of my mis - takes.

B
F♯7
I'm tel - lin my friends in - clud - in' my wife, (and everybody else)

E7
B
not fat - tnin' no more frogs for snakes.

Harmonica key of C

I Hate To See You Go

By Walter Jacobs

Cross harp

Verse 2
sire. Came home this mor - nin' 'bout half past
four, found ___ that note __________ lyin' on my
floor, "Gone a - way leave you," just don't know.
Heard ____ some bad talk, some - thing that you
said, some - thing that you said,
some - thing that you said.
Verse 3
Come on back
ba - by, hon - ey please don't go. Well, I love
you, you'll nev - er know, you'll nev - er
know, you'll nev - er know, you'll nev - er

Verse 5: Come on back, baby,
don't do no wrong,
you know I love you,
please come back home
come on back home,
come on back home, etc. to fade

Harmonica key of B♭ | Cross harp

Help Me

By Ralph Bass and Sonny Boy Williamson

B♭m
Fm
I'll have to find __ my - self, some - bod - y else
I may have to
wash,
may have to sew; I may have to cook,
I might _
___ mop the floor, but you, ___
B♭m
help me babe.
Fm
C7
You know if you don't help me dar - ling,
B♭m
Fm
I'll find my - self some - bod - y else.
Solo
B♭m

Fm
C7
B♭m
Fm
When I
walk, you walk with me, and when I talk, you talk to
B♭m
me, oh ba - by. I can't do it all by my -
Fm
C7
self, you know if you don't help me dar - ling, I have to
B♭m
Fm
find my - self some - bod - y else. Help me, help me dar - ling.
Solo

B♭m
Fm
C7
B♭m
Fm
Bring my night - shirt,
put on your morn - ing gown,
Whoa,
B♭m
Fm
bring me my night - shirt,
put on your morn - ing gown,
C7
B♭m
Dar - lin' not no way sleep - in',
but I done feel like ly - in' down,
Fm
fade ending
Oh yeah, help me.

Harmonica key of A

Honest I Do

Straight harp

By Jimmy Reed and Ewart G. Abner, Jr.

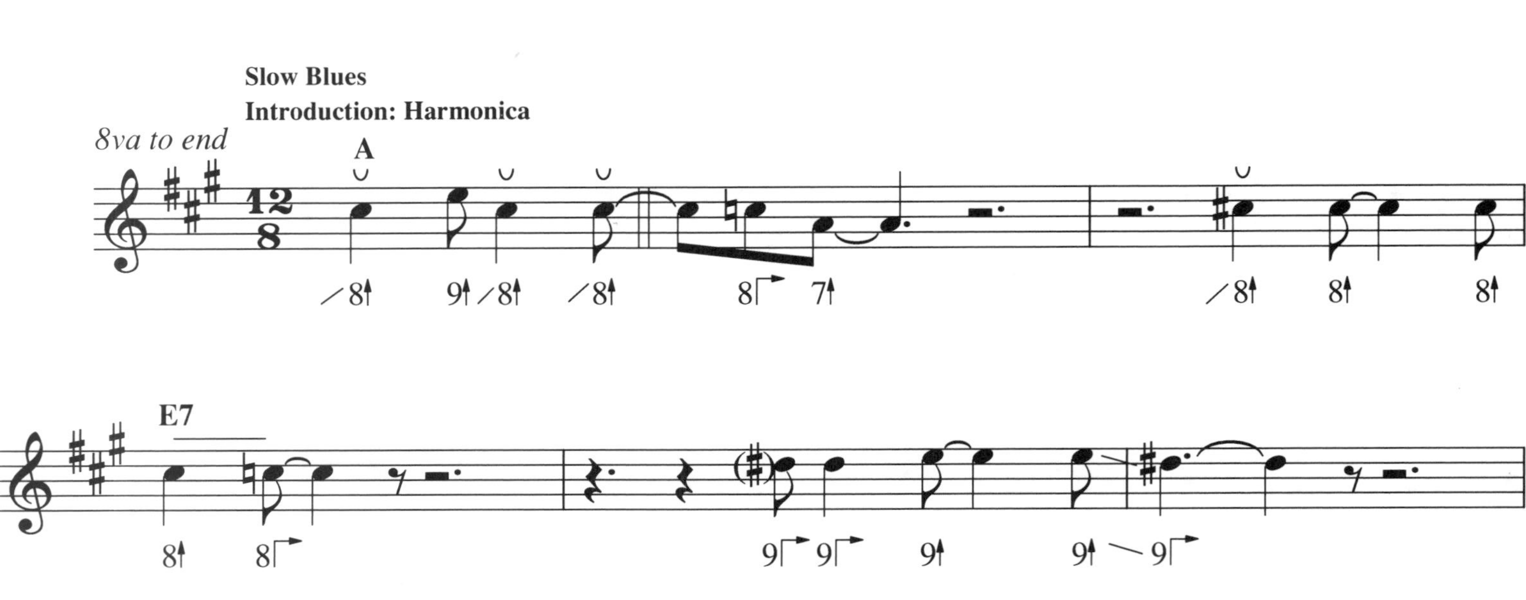

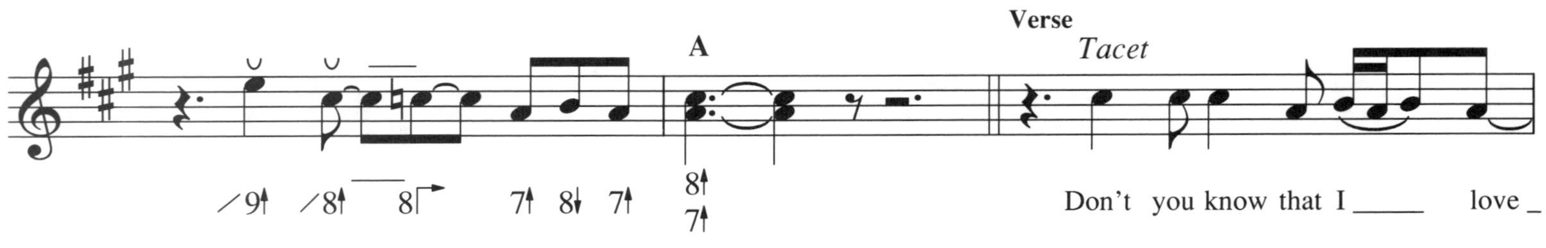

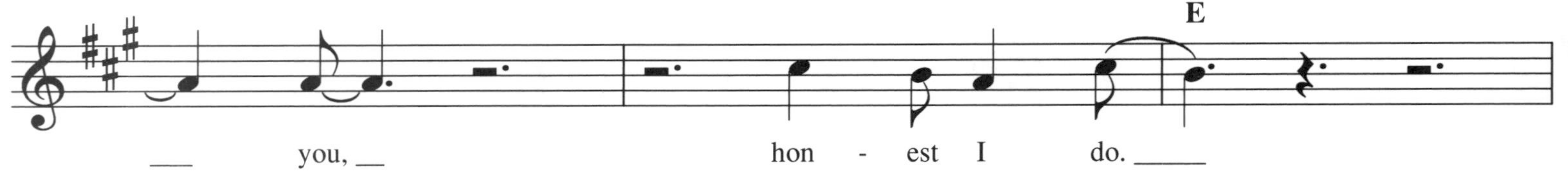

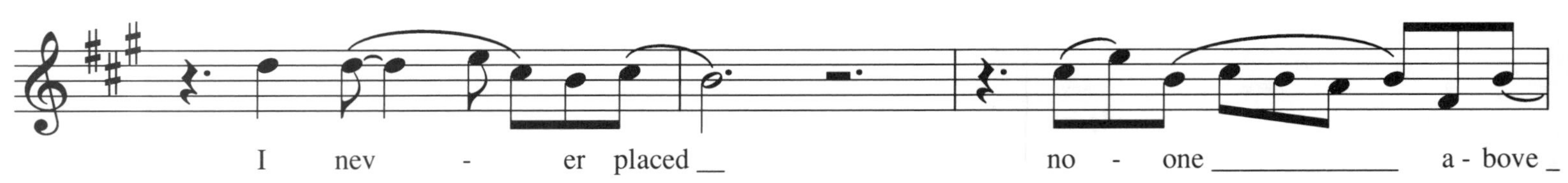

E
stop driv - in' __ me mad; ______ you're the sweet - est __ lit - tle
A
wom - an ___ that I ev - er had. ___
Harmonica Solo
↗8↑ ↗8↑ 7↑ 8↱ 7↑ 8↱ 7↑ ↗8↑ 9↑ 8↑ 9↱ 9↑ 8↑
E7
↗8↑ 8↱ 9↱ 9↑↗9↑ 9↱
Fine
9↱ 9↑ 8↑ 8↱ 7↑ 8↓ 7↑ 8↑ 7↑ 8↑ 7↑
A
I told you I _____ love _______ you, _ stop driv - in' __ me
E
mad. _______ When I woke _ up this morn - in' __
D. S. al Fine
A
nev - er felt ________ so bad. _____

Harmonica key of C

I Don't Know

By Sonny Boy Williamson

Dorian Minor (3rd position)

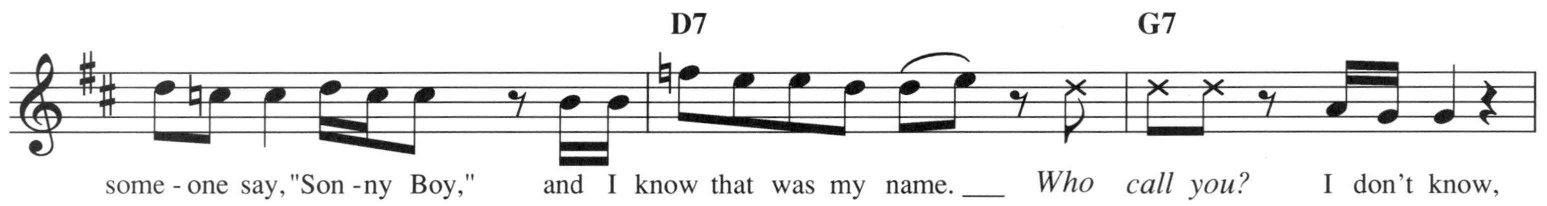

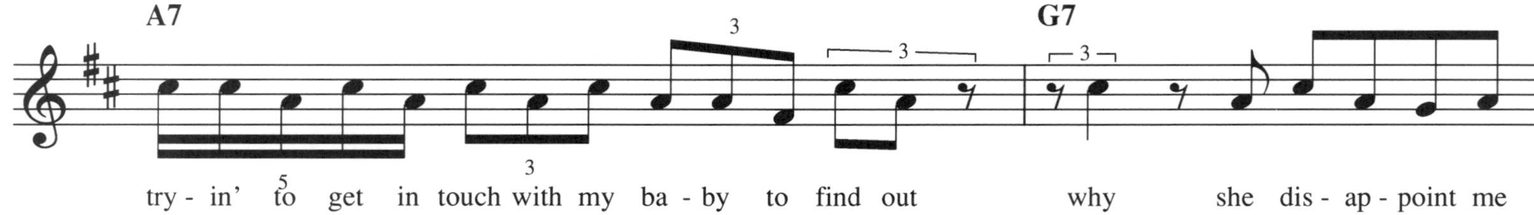

D7
G7
I wan - na know what was to blame.
I don't know.
(You mean to tell me she didn't come, man?)
D
I don't know.
But I'm
A7
G7
still try - in' to get in touch with my ba - by to find out why she dis - ap - point me
D
D
so.
2 2 3 5 4 4 3 3 2 1
I re - ceived a spec - ial de - liv - er', I re -
ceived a tel - e - gram. Then she called me long dis - tance, she wan - na' know
D7
G7
just where I am.
For what:
I don't know.
Man, I just don't
D
A7
know.
But I'm still try - in' to get in touch with my ba - by
G7
D
to find out why she dis - ap - point me so.

A7
Solo
D
That's right, that's right
D7
G7
D
A7
G7
D
A7
I know she
D
should have come by high - way, or eith - er come by rail; but she got my head in my hand,
D7
G7
won - der what's caus - in' the thrill. For what? I don't know. Man, I just don't
D
A7
know. I'm sit - tin' here won - der - in' why did my ba - by
G7
Dm7(♭5)
D
dis - ap - point me so?

Harmonica key of C

I'm A Man

By Ellas McDaniel

Cross harp

ah
ah,
ah.
All you pret - ty wo - men,
stand in line.
I can make love to ya ba - by,
in a hours time.
I'm a man,
I spell M
A
N,
man.
Solo
I'm go - in' back down
to Kan - sas to

2↓ bring ___ back a sec - ond cou - sin. 2↓ 4↑ 3↓ 3↑ 2↓ 2↓ Lit - tle John __ de Conk - e - Lou 2↓ 4↑ 3↓ 3↑ 2↓
2↓ I'm a man, ___ 2↓ 4↑ 3↓ 3↑ 2↓ 2↓ I spell M, ___ 2↓ 4↑ 3↓ 3↑ 2↓
2↓ A, ___ 2↓ 4↑ 3↓ 3↑ 2↓ 2↓ N, ___ 2↓ 4↑ 3↓ 3↑ 2↓ 2↓ man. ___ 2↓ 4↑ 3↓ 3↑ 2↓
2↓ Oh, ___ 2↓ 4↑ 3↓ 3↑ 2↓ 2↓ ah, ___ 2↓ 4↑ 3↓ 3↑ 2↓
2↓ ah, ___ 2↓ 4↑ 3↓ 3↑ 2↓ 2↓ ah. ___ 2↓ 4↑ 3↓ 3↑ 2↓
2↓ The line __ I shoot _ 2↓ 4↑ 3↓ 3↑ 2↓ 2↓ will nev - er miss. _ 2↓ 4↑ 3↓ 3↑ 2↓
2↓ The way I make love to 'em, __ 2↓ 4↑ 3↓ 3↑ 2↓ 2↓ they can't re - sist. 2↓ 4↑ 3↓ 3↑ 2↓
2↓ I'm a man, ___ 2↓ 4↑ 3↓ 3↑ 2↓ 2↓ I spell M, ___ 2↓ 4↑ 3↓ 3↑ 2↓
2↓ A, ___ 2↓ 4↑ 3↓ 3↑ 2↓ 2↓ N, ___ 2↓ 4↑ 3↓ 3↑ 2↓ 2↓ man. ___

Harmonica key of A

Juke

By Walter Jacobs

Cross harp

E
A7
E
B7
A7
E
B7
E
A7
E
B7
A7
E
B7
E

A7
E
B7
A7
E
B7
E
A7
E
B7
A7
E
B7
E

A7
E
B7
A7
E
B7
E
A7
E
B7
A7
E

Harmonica key of D

Cross harp

Just Your Fool

By Walter Jacobs

A7
D7
A
E7
D7
A
D
A
D
You must be tryin' to drive __ me crazy, treat - in' me the way __ you
A
D
A
do. I ask you please have ___ mer- cy ba - by, _______ let me
E7
A
be hap - py to you. If you're gon - na leave me for some - one
A7
D7
new, gon - na buy me a shot - gun, shoot dead at you. I ain't
A
E7
A
E7
D.S. al Coda
ly - in' no __ use of jiv - in', I'm just your fool. I'm just your
Coda
A
fool.

Harmonica key of D

Keep It To Yourself

Cross harp

By Sonny Boy Williamson

D7 A
and don't men - tion it to no - bod - y else.
E7 Solo A
D7
A
E7 D7 A
E A E
Don't tell your moth - er, don't tell your fath - er,
A E A A7
don't tell your sis - ter, don't men - tion it to your broth - er.
D7
Please ___ dar - lin', ___ keep our busi - ness to your - self. ___

A
E7
Don't you tell no - bod - y,
D7
A
and don't men- tion it to no - bod - y else.
E7
Solo
A
A7
D7
A
D7
A
E7
D7
A
E7
D7
A
E
A
E
A
(spoken)
E
You have a hus - band, I have a wife; if you start to talk that will

A
A7
D7
mess up our lives. Please, please, ba - by,
keep our busi - ness to your - self.
A
Don't you tell no - bod - y,
E7
D7
don't make it to no - bod - y else.
A
E7
(spoken) *Good - bye darlin'.*
Solo
A
A7
D7
A
E7
D7
A

Harmonica key of F

The Key

By Sonny Boy Williamson

Cross harp

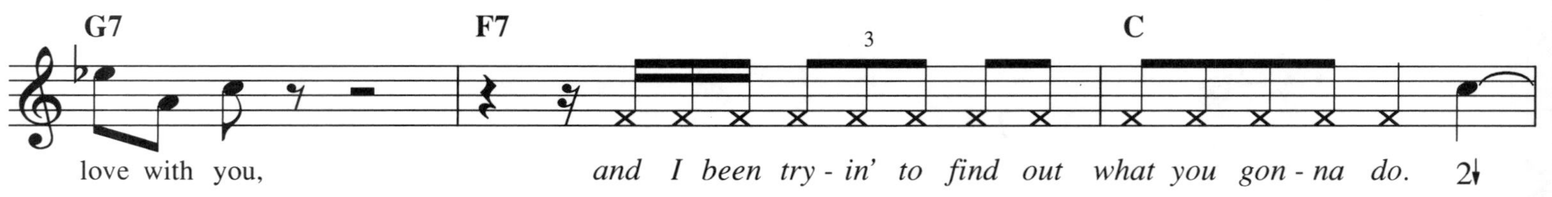

C
I know that you don't know.
G7
F7
C
All I want from you is the key to your door.
G7
C
You know I called you yes - ter - day, a
C7
F7
quar - ter af - ter nine;
I called you yes - ter - day,
C
a quar-ter af - ter nine.
But the
G7
F7
land - la - dy told me "Son - ny Boy, that wom - an gon - na cause you to lose your mine." _
C
G7
Solo
C

C7 F7
C G7
F7 C
G7 C
I called my ba - by back, fif - teen af - ter four;
C7 F7
I called my ba - by back, fif - teen af - ter four.
C G7
I'm just ask - in' you please, please dar - lin',
F7 C
give me the key to your door.

Harmonica key of A

Ice Cream Man

By John Brim

Straight harp

A7
need some - thing to keep you cool.
Now,
D7
A
sum - mer - time is here, need some - thing to keep you cool.
E7
D7
Hey, lit - tle girl,
I've got some - thing for
you.
I'm your ice cream man,
stop me when I'm pass - ing by.
I'm your

D7
A
ice cream man,
stop me when I'm passing by.
E7
D7
Now, I'd cool you off, little girl,
guarantee I'll satisfy.
A
E7
A
I got cream sandwiches,
Dixie cups,
popsicles and push-ups too.
A7
I'm your
D7
A
ice cream man,
stop me when I'm passing by.

E7
D7
Now, I cool you of, lit - tle girl, ___ guar - an - tee I'll sat - is -
E7
D7
4 3 3 2 2 2 2
A
E7
fy.
Solo
A
E7
A
1 2 2 2 4 2 2 2 2 2 2 2 2 2
A7
D7
A7
D7
2 2 2 2 2 2 2 2 2 2 2 2
A
A
2 2 2 2 2 2 2 2 2 2 2
E7
D7
A
E7
I
E7
D7
A
E7
2 2 2 2 2 2 2 2 1 2 2 2 2 3 2

I've got all flavors
including pineapple too
I've got all flavors
including pineapple too
Now one of my flavors little girl
has got to be the right for you

Harmonica key of C

Let Me Explain

Cross harp

By Sonny Boy Williamson

C7 G D7
I'll al - ways __ be your man. ___ 2↓ 2↓ 2↓ 2↓ 1↓ 1↓ Let's
G
love a lit - tle, and kiss a lit - tle, you lay back in my arms; _
C7
___ let's love a lit - tle, and kiss a lit - tle, and lay
G D7
way back in my arms. ___ I wan - na ex - plain to you ba - by,
C7 G D7
just how much you treat me wrong. _ 2↓ 2↓ 2↓ 2↓ 2↓ 2↓ 1↓ 1↓ 1↓
Solo
G
2↓ 3↓ 2↓ 2↓ 3↓ 3↓ 2↓ 2↓ 3↓ 2↓ 2↓ 4↓
G7 C7
4↓ 3↓ 3↓ 3↓ 2↓ 2↓ 3↓ 3↓ 3↓ 2↓ 2↓ 2↑ 2↓
G D7
3↓ 3↓ 2↓ 2↑ 2↓ 2↑ 3↓ 2↓ 1↓ 3↓ 3↓ 2↓ 3↓ 2↓ 3↓ 2↓ 3↓ 2↓ 3↓

C7 G D7 G
Whoa, ba - by, 'low
me a chance to ex - plain; oh
C7 G
ba - by, oh ba - by, 'low me a chance to ex - plain.
D7 C7
I love you for my girl - friend, why can't I be your
G D7 G
man? There's noth - in' in the world that
I would - n't do for you; and there's
C7 G
noth - in' in the world that I would not do for you.
D7 C7
Don't you know I love you, how come you can't love me

G D7 G
too? We gon - na kiss a lit - tle, we gon - na
hug a lit - tle, lay way back in my arms; we gon - na
C7 G
kiss a lit - tle, we gon - na love a lit - tle, and lay way back in my
D7 C7
arms. I wan - na ex - plain to you ba - by that I nev - er will do you
G D7 G
wrong.
G7 C7
G D7
C7 G

Harmonica key of C

Let Your Conscience Be Your Guide

Cross harp

By Sonny Boy Williamson

G
G7
C7
G
D7
C7
G
D7
G
You're the same lit - tle wom - an, well
C7
G
so nice, lov - in', kind to me in ev - er - y way.
C7
You are the same lit - tle wom - an well
G
so nice, lov - in', kind to me in ev - er - y way;
D7
but if you nev - er lie to me, I'll be by your

C7 G D7
side ___ both night and day. You have a
G C7 G
strong _________ con - sti - tu - tion, and I'm not gon - na let you down.;
C7
you have a strong ________ con - sti - tu - tion, and I'm not gon - na let you down. __
G D7
And if you nev - er lie __ to me dar - lin', I'll
C7 G D7
al - ways be a - round and I won't let you down.
Yeah, man.
G G7
C7 G
D7 C7 G

Harmonica key of C

Off The Wall

By Jimmy Reed

Cross harp

G D7 C7
G D7 G
G7 C7
G D7 C7
G D G
C7
G D7 C7
G D7 G

C7
G
D7
drum solo
G
G7
C7
G
D7
C7
G
D7
G
G7
C7
G
D7
C7
G

Mean Old World

Harmonica key of B♭ | Cross harp

By Walter Jacobs

B♭7
F
gon - na pack my bags ___ and go. ______
Yes, ______
I've got the blues, ___
gon - na pack my things __ and go. _____
C7
Well, I guess you don't love me, _____
you love that mis - ter so - and - so __
Solo
F7
D. S. al Coda
Coda
so.

Harmonica key of F

Nine Below Zero

By Sonny Boy Williamson

Cross harp

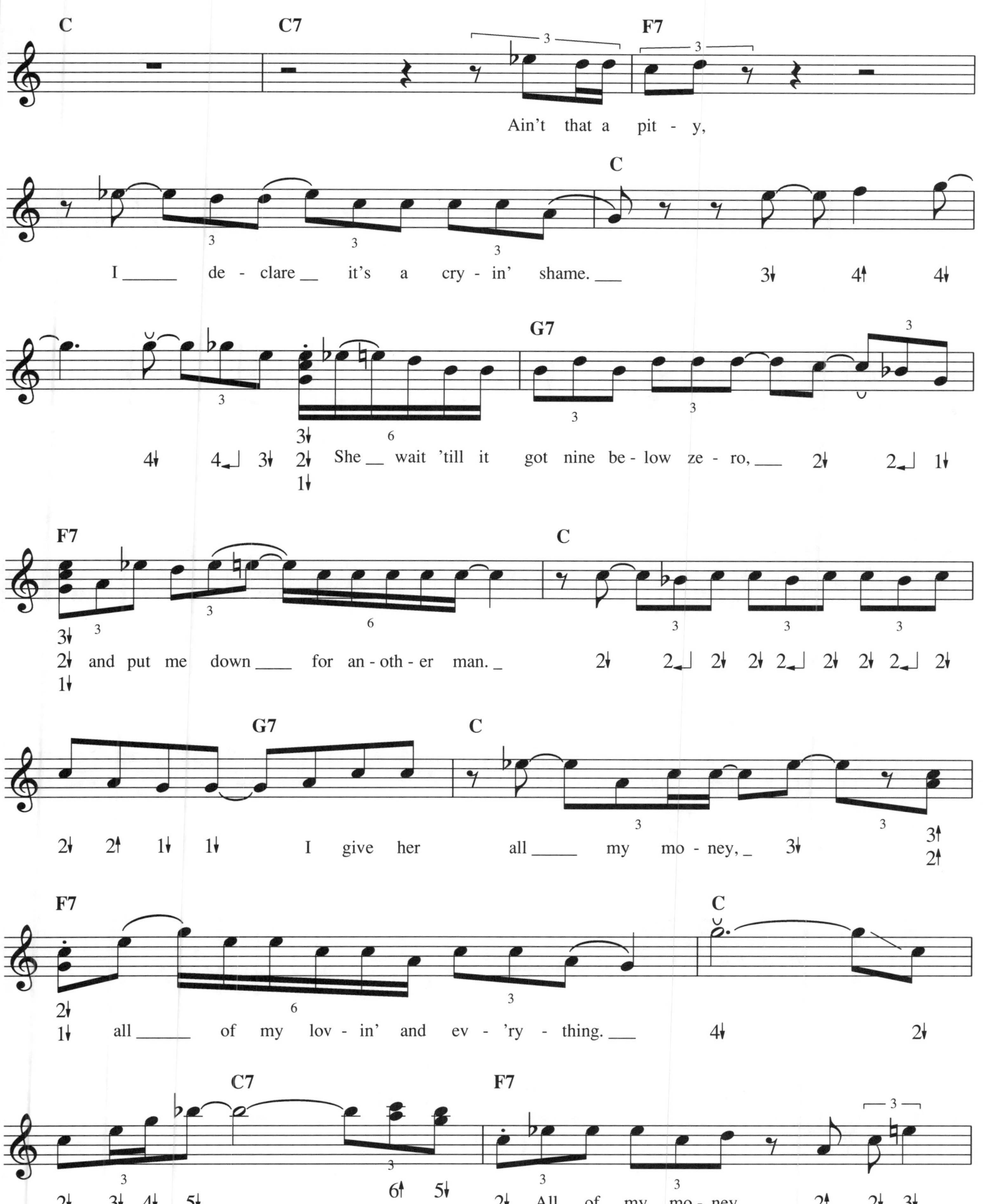
C
C7
F7
Ain't that a pit - y,
C
I ___ de - clare ___ it's a cry - in' shame. ___ 3↓ 4↑ 4↓
G7
4↓ 4 3↓ 3↓ 2↓ 1↓ She ___ wait 'till it got nine be - low ze - ro, ___ 2↓ 2 1↓
F7
C
3↓ 2↓ 1↓ and put me down ___ for an - oth - er man. ___ 2↓ 2 2↓ 2↓ 2 2↓ 2↓ 2 2↓
G7
C
2↓ 2↑ 1↓ 1↓ I give her all ___ my mo - ney, ___ 3↓ 3↑ 2↑
F7
C
2↓ 1↓ all ___ of my lov - in' and ev - 'ry - thing. ___ 4↓ 2↓
C7
F7
2↓ 3↓ 4↓ 5↓ 6↑ 5↑ 5↓ 4↓ 2↓ All of my mo - ney, 2↑ 2↓ 3↓

all of my love-ly love in vain.
C
G7
Nine below zero,
F7
and she done put me down for an-oth-er man.
C
G7
Solo
C
F7
C
C7
F7
C
G7

F7
C
G7
C
All ___ of my mo - ney,
F7
all ___ of my lov - in' and ev - 'ry - thing. _
C
F7
All my mo - ey, ___
all my lov - in' and ev - 'ry - thing. _______
C
Yes, it's nine be - low ze - ro. _____ She done
G7
F7
put __ me down _ for an-oth - er man.
C

Harmonica key of B♭

Ninety Nine

By Sonny Boy Williamson

Cross harp

Fast shuffle

Solo
C7
F
4 4 4 4 3 4 4 4 4 4 4 3
F7
B♭7
4 4 3 2 2 2 2 2 2
F
C7
4 4 3 4 4 4 3 4 4 4 3 3
B♭7
F
C7
3 4 3 3 2 2 2 2 1 1
Yes, I'm in
F
B♭7
love with the lit - tle girl, just be - cause she's so nice and
F
B♭7
kind. I'm in love, I'm in love with the lit - tle girl,
F
just be - cause she's so nice and kind. I was so sor - ry when she

C7
B♭7
F
asked me for one hun-dred dol-lars;
I could-n't give her but nine - ty - nine.
C7
Solo
F
B♭7
F
F7
B♭7
F
C7
B♭7
F
C7
F
B♭7
Yes, my ba - by tak - en sick on Ju - ly the twen - ty -
F
B♭7
ninth.
Yeah, the one I love, she tak - en sick, boys

F
on Ju - ly the twen - ty - ninth. __
Her doc - tor bill was
C7
B♭7
four hun - dred dol - lars, and I didn't have but three hun - dred and nine - ty -
F
C7
Solo
F
nine. __
B♭7
F
F7
B♭7
F
C7
B♭7
F
B♭7 F

Harmonica key of D

One Way Out

Cross harp

By Sonny Boy Williamson, Elmore James and Marshall Sehorn

ba - by; I just can't go out that
door. You know there ain't but
D7
one way out wom - an; I just
can't go out that door.
3
A
3↓ 2↓ 1↓ 3↑ 2↑ 1↑ 3↑ 2↑ 1↑ 2↓ 1↓ 3↑ 2↑
3↓ 2↓ 1↓ 3↓ 2↓ 1↓ 3↑ 2↑ 1↑ 2↓ 1↓ 3↓ 2↓ 1↓
E7
I see a man down -
D7
stairs might be your man, I don't
A
know. Now, you
got me trapped wom - an, up on the sec - ond

floor. If I get a - way this time, I won't be
D7
trapped no more. So you raise your
3
win - dow so I can ease out soft and
A
slow.
E7
3
D7
None of your neigh - bors won't be talk - in' that
A
stuff that they don't know.
Solo

D7
A
E7
D7
A
Oh, there ain't but
one way out __ lit - tle girl,
and I just can't go

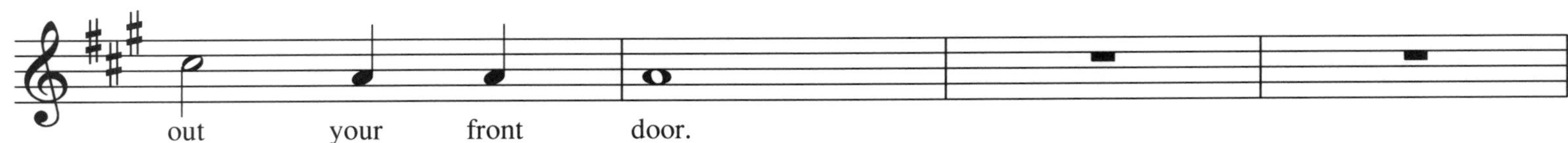
out your front door.

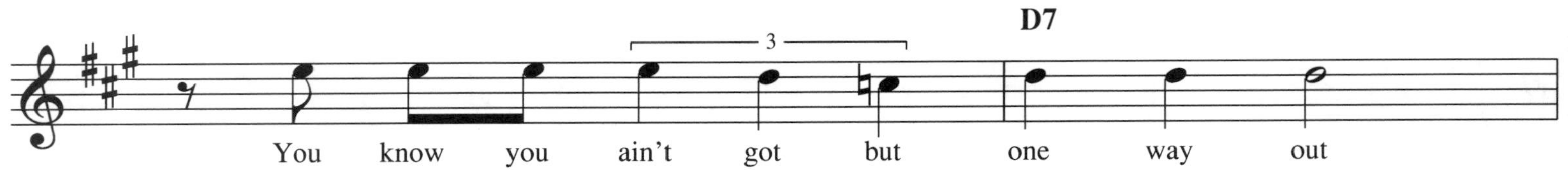
D7
3
You know you ain't got but one way out

ba - by, and I just can't go out that door.

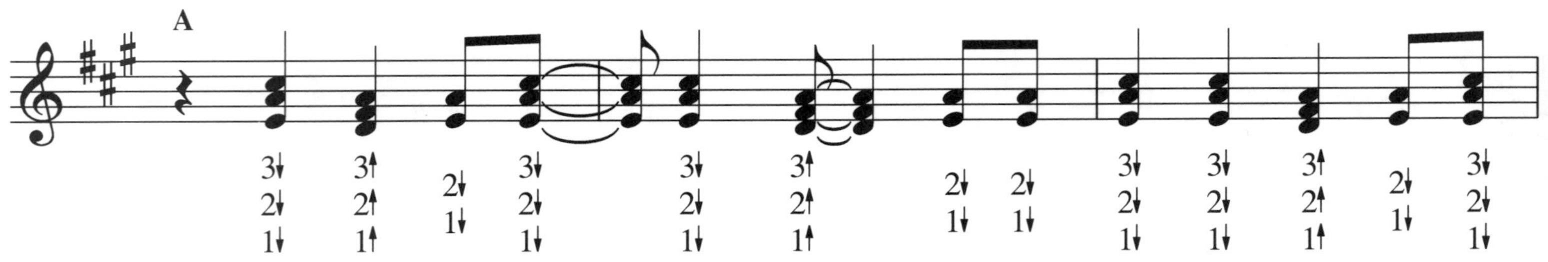
A

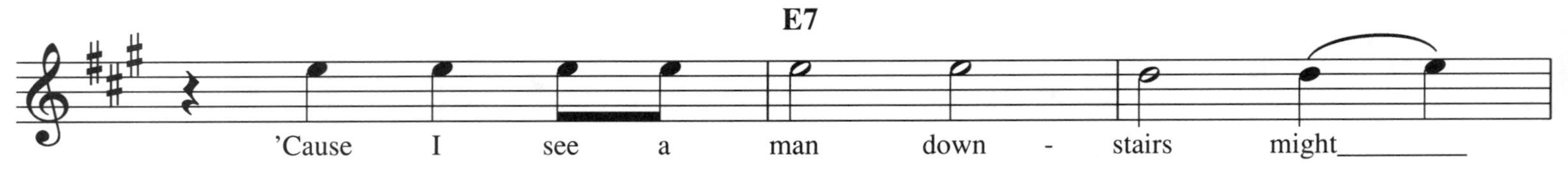
E7
'Cause I see a man down - stairs might

D7
A
be your man, I don't know.

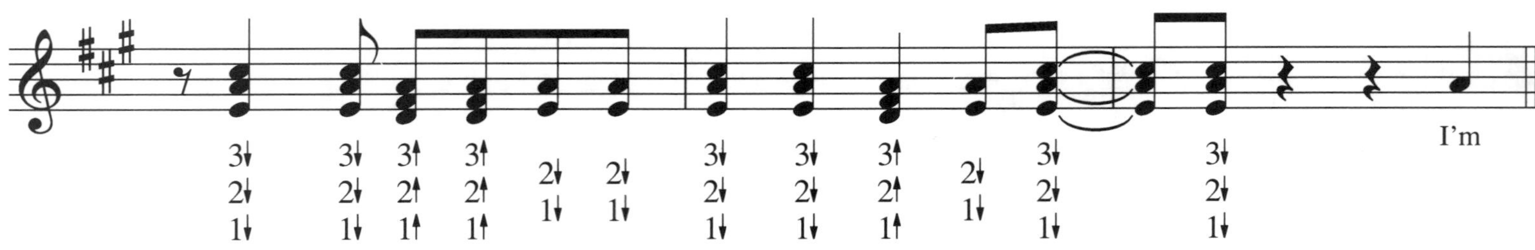
I'm

fool - ish to be in here in the first place. ____
I know __ some - one else gon - na' walk in, take my
D7
place, but ain't no way in the world ___
A
I'm ______ go - in' ______ out that ____ door. __________
See, a
E7
D7
man down - stairs might be your
A
man, I don't know. ___
Fade ending

Rattlesnake

Harmonica key of A

By John Brim

Cross harp

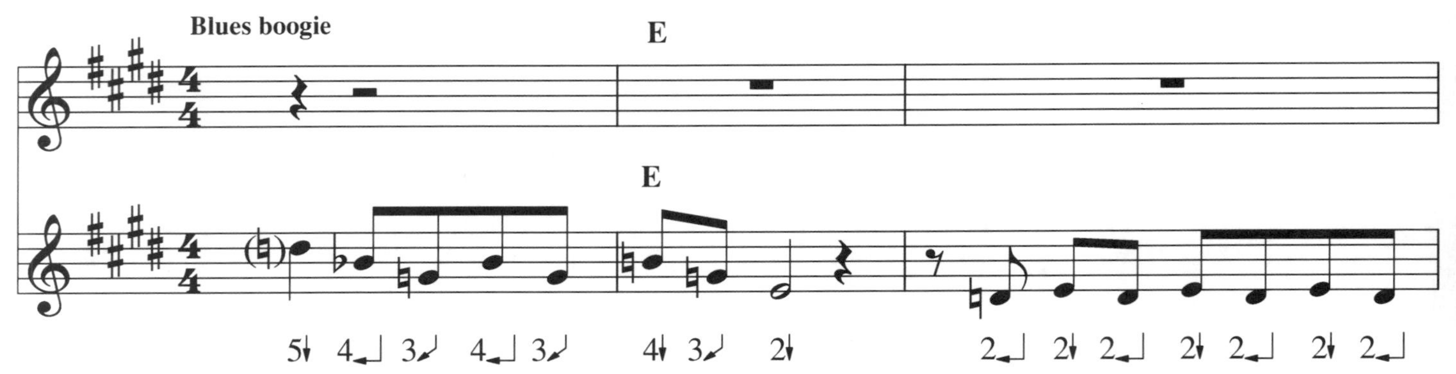

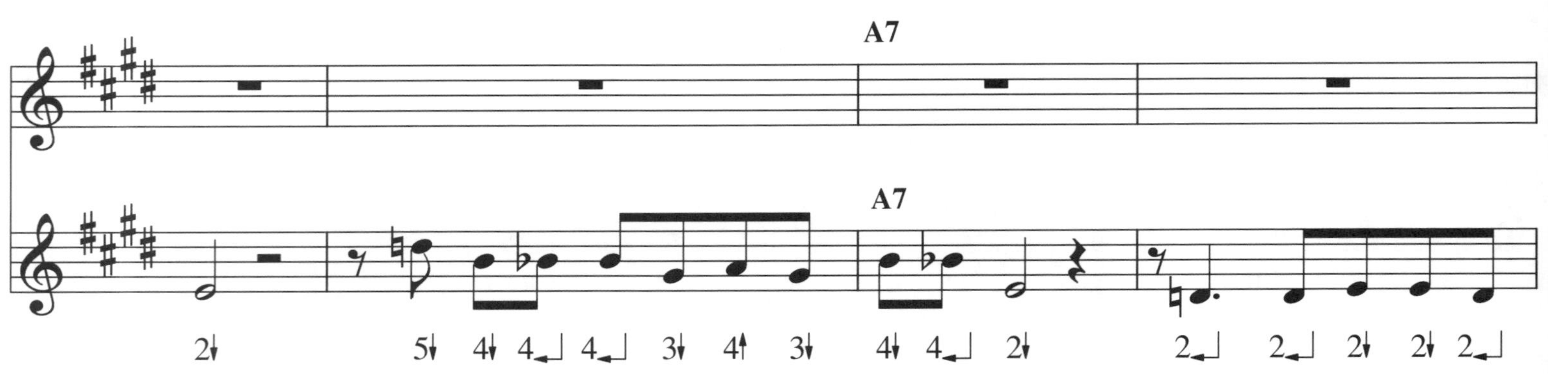

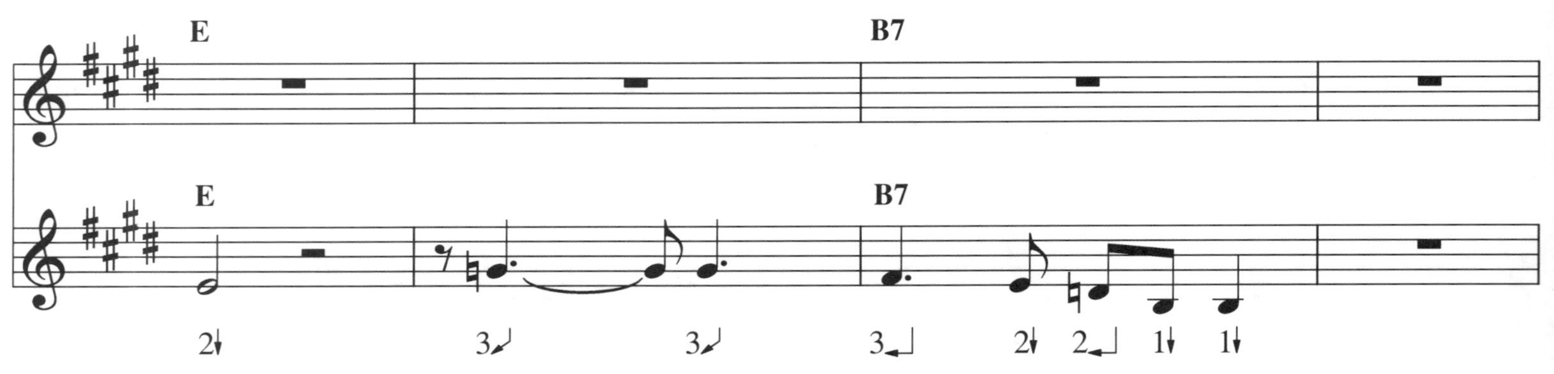

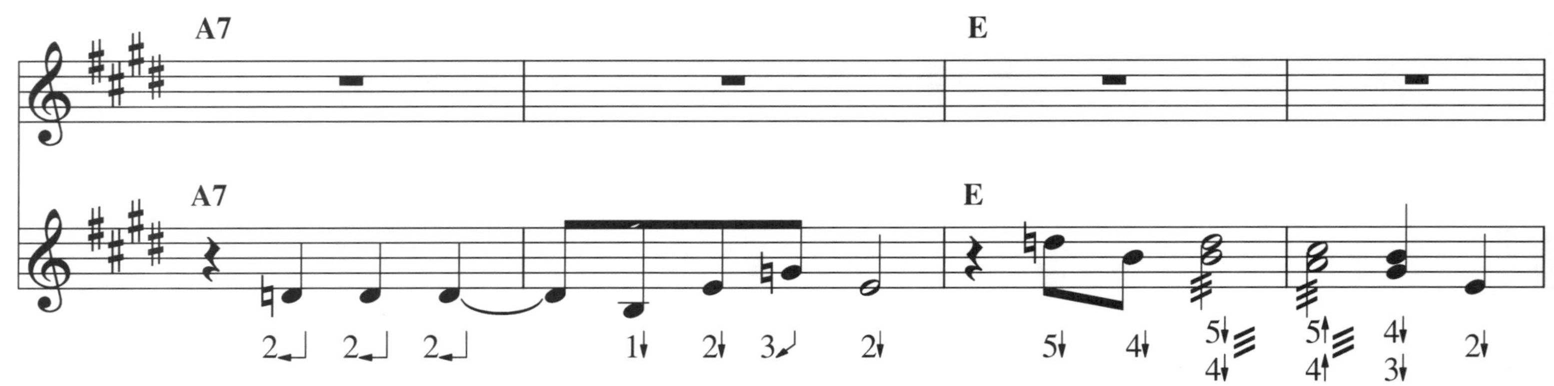

B7
You ain't noth - ing but a rat - tle - snake,
B7
2 2 1 1 4 4 3 2 2 2
come craw - lin' round my door.
2 2 2 2 2 2 4 4 3 2 2 2
A7
Noth - ing but a rat - tle - snake, come craw - lin' round my
A7
5 4 3 4 3 4 4 3 2 2 2 2 2 2
E
B7
door. You wear your tail,
E
B7
2 2 2 2 2 2 2 3 3 3 2 2 1 1
A7
E
you ain't goin' fight me no more.
A7
E
1 2 2 2 1 2 1

They told me you was out there;
I couldn't see your face.
They told me you was out there,
A7
A7
E
I couldn't even see your face.
E
I could

B7
A7
E
hear you, ba - by, wav - in' round your tail.
B7
A7
E
3 2 2 1 1 1 2 2 2
B7
You ain't
B7
2 1 2 1 2 1 1 1 1 1 2 2 2 1 1
E
noth - ing but a rat - tle - snake, come craw - lin' 'round my door.
E
5 4 4 5 4
You ain't noth - ing but a rat - tle - snake,
A7
A7
5 4 4 3 5 4
come craw - ling round my door.
4 3 2 2 2 3 2 3 2 2 1 1 1

E
B7
Yes, I'm sure ______ you
A7
E
ain't goin' bite ______ me no more. ______
B7
E
A7

You make me feel so good;
you make me weep and moan.
You make me feel so good;
you make me weep and moan.
You ain't lookin' for nothing;
you just lookin' for a home.

Harmonica key of B♭

Cross harp

Sitting On Top Of The World

By Chester Burnett

C7 B♭7 C7 F B♭7
because I'm sitting on top of the world.
F C7 Solo F F7
B♭7 B♭m7 F
B♭7 C7 F B♭7
F C7 F
Goin' down to the freight yard, chasin' me a freight train.
F7 B♭7
I'm gon' leave this town, work done got
B♭m7 F C7
hard. But now she's gone and I don't worry,
B♭7 C7 F B♭7 F B♭7 F
sitting on top of the world.

Harmonica key of A

Smokestack Lightning

By Chester Burnett

Cross harp

Fast shuffle

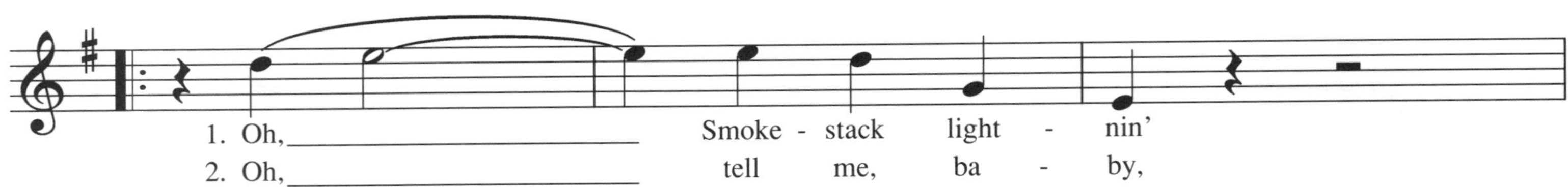

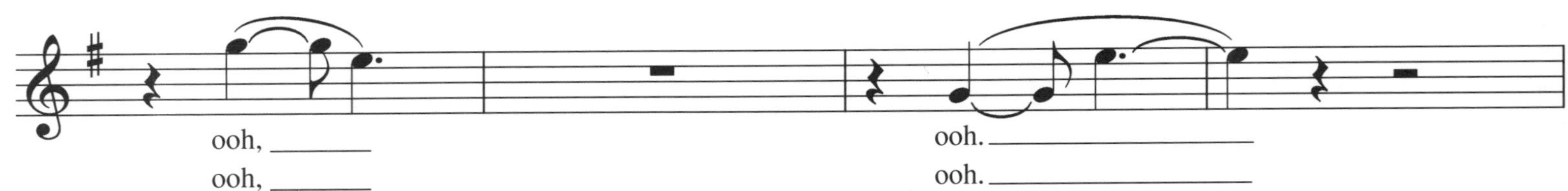

1.
2.
3. Whoa, ___ tell me, baby where did you stay last night? ___ Oh, don't you hear me cry - in'?
4. Whoa, ___ stop your train, ___ let a ___ poor boy ride. ___
Ooh, ___ ooh, ___ ooh. ___
1.

2.
5. Whoa, fare - you well,
6. Whoa, who's been here ba - by since
nev - er see you no mo'.
I been gone, lit - tle bit - ty boy.
Oh, don't you hear me cry - in'?
Ooh, ooh, woo.
1.
3
2.
repeat to fade

Octave-low harmonica key of C

Unseen Eye

By Sonny Boy Williamson

Cross harp

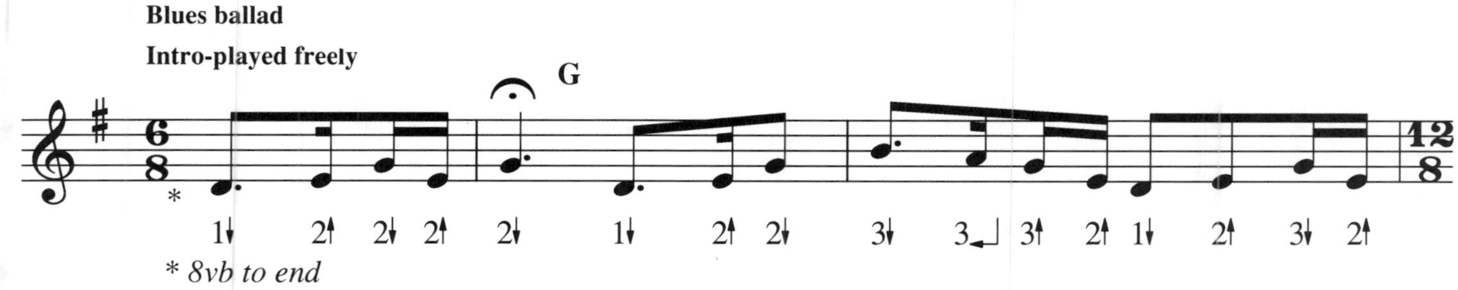

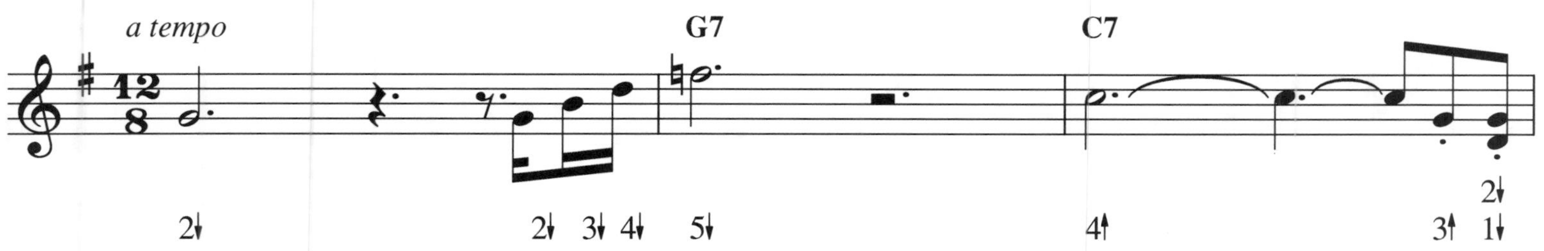

* *Harmonica part is performed one octave lower than written.*

D7
G
6
1
I'm beg - gin' Miss Min - nie Bell
C7
G
to be care-ful __ at what you do. ____
I am
C7
beg - gin' Miss Min-nie Bell
to be care - ful in what you say or
G
D7
do.
I'm just tryin' to hip you, dar - ling,
C7
G
D7
'cause that un - seen eye ___ is watch-in' you. ___
Please
G
C7
G
don't let your right hand
know what your left hand is do - in'. _
G7
C7
Please don't let your right hand
know what your left hand do.

G
D7
I'm just tryin' to put your boots on you and hip you, wom-an,
C7
G
D7
Solo
be-cause that un - seen eye ___ is watch-in' you. ___
G
C7
G
G7
C7
G
D7
Yes, ___ I'm just tryin' to put your boots on you, wom - an,
C7
G
'cause that un - seen eye ___ is watch - in' you. ___

Harmonica key of B♭

Too Close Together

By Sonny Boy Williamson

Cross harp

* *Long note is sustained as indicated through right side of mouth; chords are played by lifting tongue rhythmically on and off harmonica.*

C7
F
3↓ 2↓ I had two fine chicks, lived both there on the same street.
B♭7
So much love at a time could-n't be beat it was too close to - geth - er.
F
Yes man, they lived too close to - geth - er. Yeah, they lived
C7
B♭7
so close to - geth - er that I could - n't see one for the
F
C7
oth - er.
F
Ear - ly one Sun-day mor-nin' they both would go to church I tried to slip on out, but I
B♭7
see it just won't work. It was too close to - geth-er, yeah, it was

F
C7
too close to - geth - er.
3↓ 2↓
3↑ 2↓
2↑ 1↓
I know we're too close to-geth - er and I

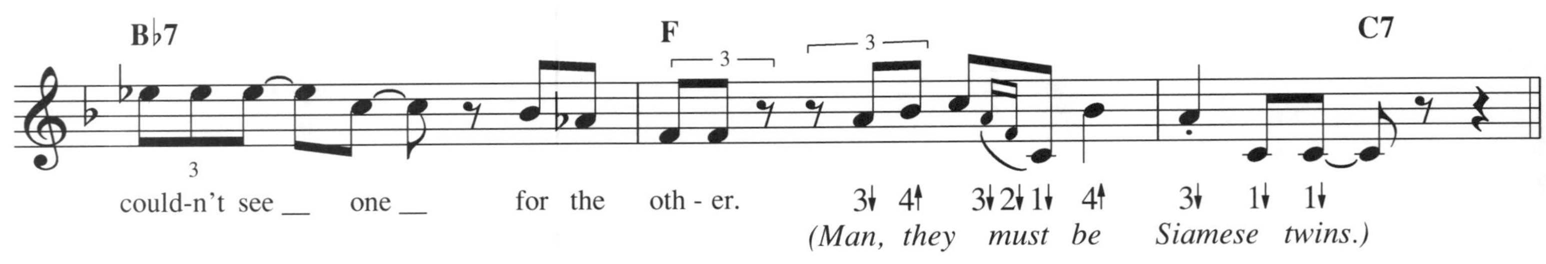
B♭7
F
C7
could-n't see __ one __ for the oth - er.
3↓ 4↑ 3↓ 2↓ 1↓ 4↑ 3↓ 1↓ 1↓
(Man, they must be Siamese twins.)

Solo
F
2↓ 2↓ 3↓ 2↓ 3↓ 4↑ 4↓ 3↓ 2↓ 2↑ 2↓ 2↓ 3↓

F7
B♭7
F
4↓ 3↓ 2↓ 3↓ 3 2↓ 3↓ 3 2↓ 2↓ 2↑ 3↓ 4↓ 3↓

C7
B♭7
3↓ 3↓ 4↓ 5↓ 4↓ 4↓ 3↓ 4↓ 5↓ 4↑ 3↓ 2↓ 3↑ 2↑ 4↓

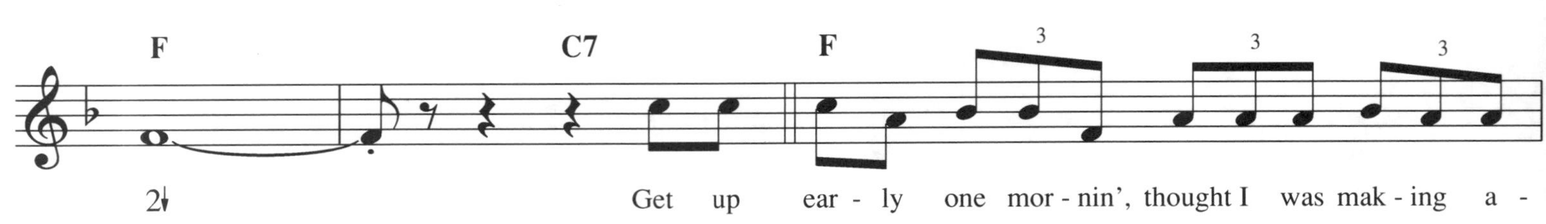
F
C7
F
2↓
Get up ear - ly one mor - nin', thought I was mak - ing a -

'fore ___ day creep. Time I knocked on her door, the oth - er girl said,
"Is you look-in' for me?" __ It was too close to-geth-er; whoa, yes __ it was
too close to - geth - er. I know it was too close to-geth - er and I
could - n't see one ___ for see - in' the oth - er.
Bb7
F
C7
Fade

Harmonica key of D

Walkin' By Myself

By James A. Lane

Cross harp

E7
A
I love you, yes, I love you
with all my heart and soul.
A7
D7
I would - n't mis - treat you
E7
A
E7
for my weight in gold.
Bridge: stop time
A
You know I love you, you know it's

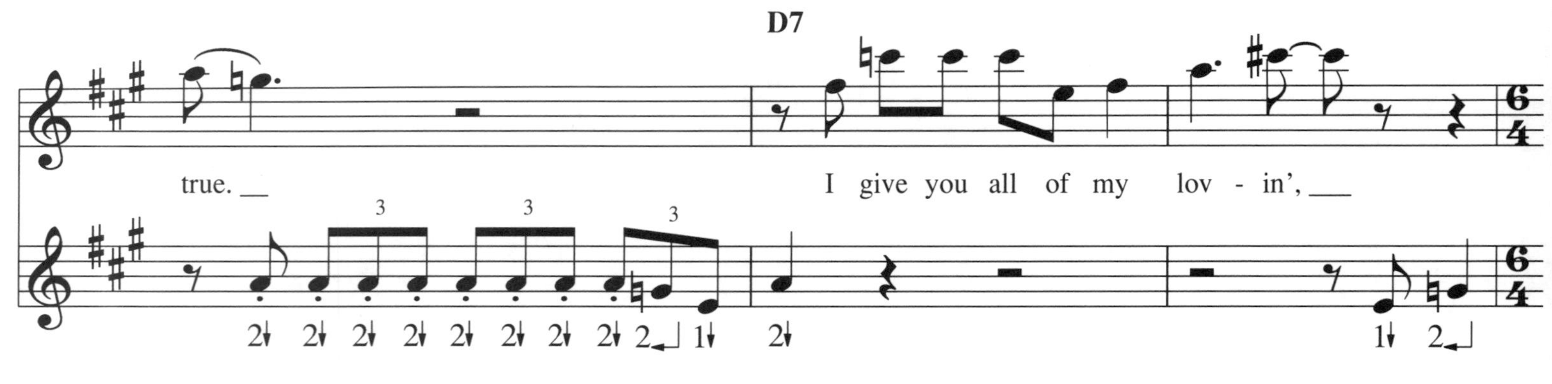
D7
true. __
I give you all of my lov - in', ___
2 2 2 2 2 2 2 2 2 1 2
1 2

E7
A
what more ___ can I do? ____
Walk - in'
2
2 3 4 5

A7
by my - self, I hope you un - der - stand. ______
5 4 4 3 6
5
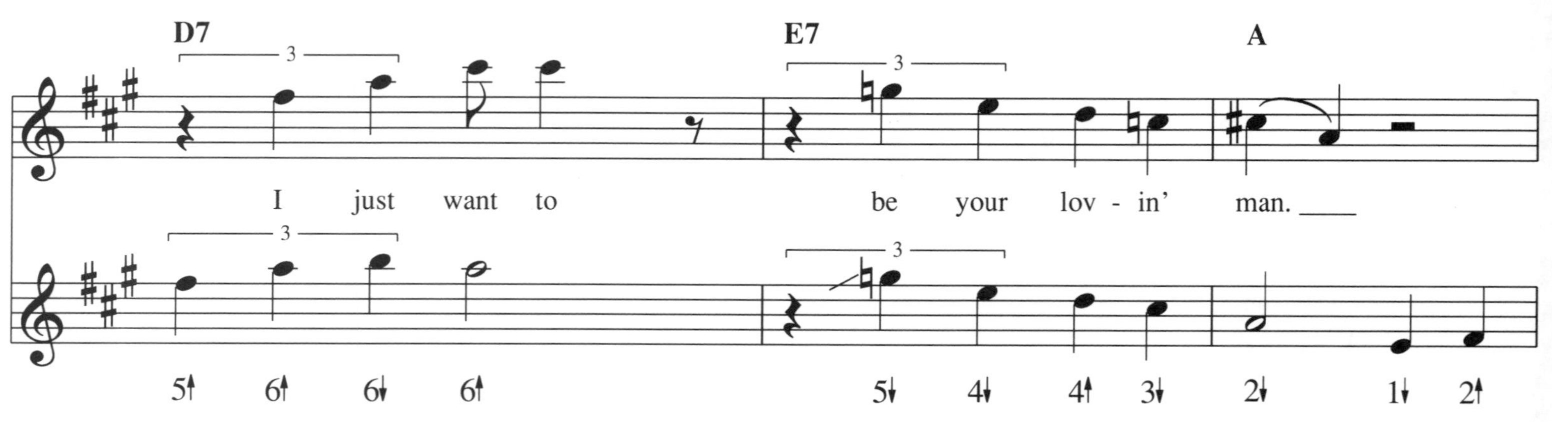
D7
E7
A
I just want to be your lov - in' man. ____
5 6 6 6 5 4 4 3 2 1 2

E7
Solo
A
2 1 1
2 2 2 2 2 2 2 2 2 2 2 2 2
2 2 2 2 2 2 2 2 2 2 2 2

A7
D7
A
E7
D7
A
E7
A
A7
D7
A
E7
D7
A
E7

Harmonica key of A

Cross harp

You're So Fine

By Walter Jacobs

B7 A7 E
fine pret - ty ba - by, let - tin' me love you __ all the time. ____
B7 E
Well, I will just give you all my mon - ey, buy you
dia-monds ev - 'ry thing, 'til you'll be mine, ba - by, we will nev - er miss. You ____
A7 E
__ so fine, ____ yeah, ____ you so fine; you a
B7 A7 E
fine heal - thy thing. I want to love you all the time. __
B7 E
E7 A7
E

B7
A7
E
5 5 4 4 3 2
3 3 2 2 1 1 1 2

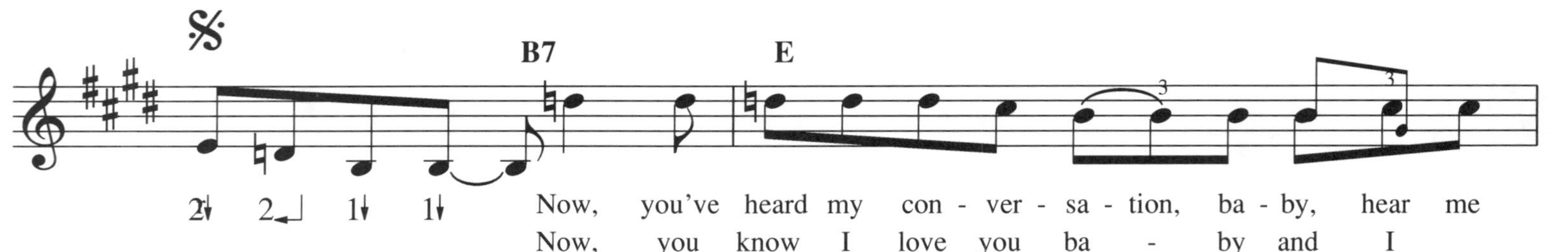
B7
E
2 2 1 1
Now, you've heard my con - ver - sa - tion, ba - by, hear me
Now, you know I love you ba - by and I

talk my - self to death; I'm in love with you ba - by and I don't
just can't help my - self; I'm go - in' craz - y 'cause you lov - in'

A7
want no - bod - y else,
some - one else,
You so fine,

E
yeah you so fine.
2
2
You a
You a

B7
A7
to Coda
E
fine heal - thy thing, I want to love you all the time
fine heal - thy thing, let me love you all the
2

B7
E
2 2 1
2 3 3 2
3 2 2 2

A7
E
Yeah,
B7 A7 E D. S. al Coda
you so fine ba-by, let me love you all the time.
Coda
E B7 E
time.
A7 E
B7 A7
E

Harmonica key of D

You Killing Me

By Sonny Boy Williamson

Straight harp

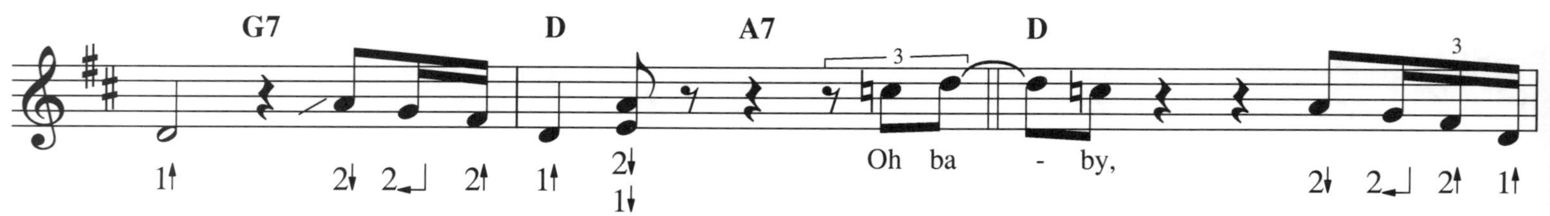

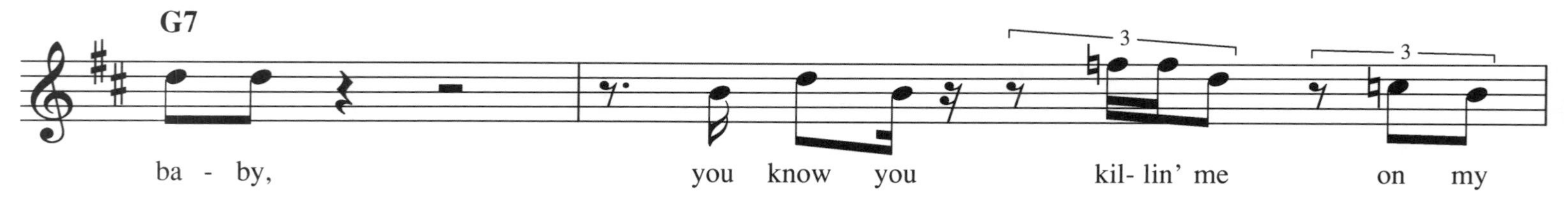

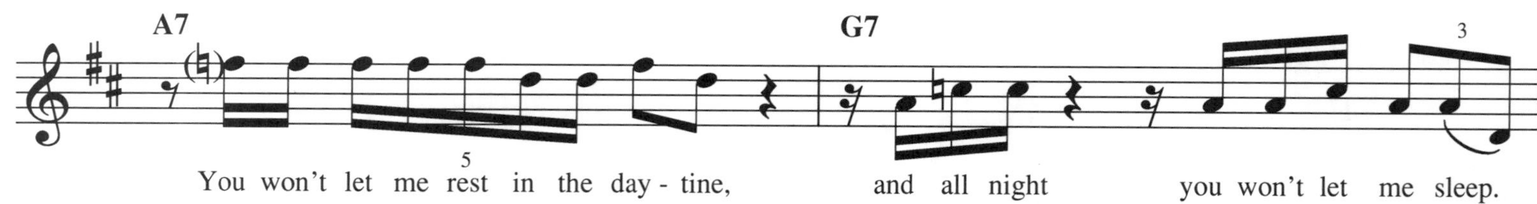

D
A7
But the lit - tle
D
G7
girl she came to me one ___ morn' __
and said, "Son- ny Boy, ______ I a - pol - o - gize."
D
D7
G7
Mmm. _________
Come to me one morn',
and said, "Son - ny Boy, ___ I a - pol - o - gize." _____
D
A7
Say I told the lit - tle girl I'm goin' for - give you ba - by,
G7
D
so you can have one ___ more try. ________
A7
Solo
D
G7
D
G7

D
A7
G7
D
A7
D
It's one thing ba - by now real - ly,
I want you to do.
Treat me nice, ma - ma, and I won't
D7
love no - bod - y but you.
G7
Treat me kind,
and there's noth - ing
I wouldn't do,
D
A7
Come home now, dar - lin', I won't
G7
love no - bod - y but you.
D

Harmonica key of G

Your Funeral And My Trial

Cross harp

By Sonny Boy Williamson

G7
D
A7
got - ta be your fu - ner - al ___ and my trial.
When I and you

D
first got to - geth - er, it was on one Fri - day night. We spent two love - ly hours _ to - geth - er, and the

G7
world knew it was all - right. I'm just beg - gin' you, ba - by, please cut out that

D
A7
off the wall jive,
You know you got to treat me bet - ter, if you

G7
D
A7
don't it's got to be your __ fun - eral and my trial.
(all right)

Solo
D
D7

G7
D

A7
G7
D
A7
4↓ 4↓ 4↓ 4↑ 5↑ 4↑ 3↑ 3↓ 3↓ 3↓ 2↓
The
D
Lord made the world and ev - 'ry - thing was in it. The way my ba - by loves is so
sol - id cen - ter. She can love to heal the sick, and she can love to raise the dead. You
G7
might think I'm jok - in' but you'd bet - ter be - lieve what I said, I'm beg - gin you ba - by,
D
cut out that off the wall jive.
3↓ 4↑ 4↓ 4 3↓ 2↓ 3↓ 2↓
A7
G7
Ei - ther you got to treat me bet - ter, it's got to be your fun - er - al and my
D
trial. 2↓ 3↓ 4↑ 4 4↓ 4↑ 3↓ 2↓ 1↓ 2↓ 2↓